Edgar Cayce's
MASSAGE
Hydrotherapy
& Healing Oils

Joseph B. Duggan, Ms.T.
Sandra Duggan, RN, Ms.T.

illustrations by Terry Cox Joseph

INNER VISION
Publishing Company
Virginia Beach, Virginia

This book is published by:

Inner Vision Publishing Co.
Box 1117, Seapines Station
Virginia Beach, VA 23451 USA
Phone: (804) 671-1777

This book is printed in the United States of America.

First Printing, January 1989

ISBN 0-917483-12-X

CONTENTS

FOREWORD

This is a long overdue book. Except for a few intrepid souls who touched the wealth of massage information in the Edgar Cayce readings, this information has lain dormant for many years. Two who persisted in the task of uncovering this important information were Joe and Sandra Duggan.

Several times our paths crossed unexpectedly. I first met Joe and Sandra at Virginia Beach. At another time while I was working with Dr. Reilly in New Jersey, Joe and Sandra stopped by for a few hours. Having accepted the request to examine the manuscript for their book, it seems as though I have met them again as I follow their searchings while they knock on the doors of the unknown and try to understand the healing process.

One of the strengths of this book is its example. It is a tangible fruit of the spirit of inquiry so encouraged in the Cayce readings. Though often discouraged by the task, Joe and Sandra used and adapted what was available to them. They sought out new knowledge, intentionally acquired new skills and persevered in their quest for understanding.

For me, the most exciting aspect of their book is Joe's discovery of Korr's work. Dr. Korr is a researcher and physiologist who began to work with osteopaths in the decades following Mr. Cayce's death. In particular, his hypotheses about the nature of the sympathetic nervous system have a ring of truth about them in light of the picture that emerges from the Cayce readings.

Talking about the readings is not the same as reading them yourself. For one interested in what the Cayce readings have to say on healthful living patterns, this book has a wealth of verbatim reading quotations about massage which have not been included together before. Though the language of the readings often seems obscure at first, carefully pondering them is a most fruitful path to new insight. I have never known this method to fail. Be patient, and listen as you read and reread the readings.

You will not go wrong if you follow the suggestions in this

book *and your intuition.* If you want to know more and to develop your own skills, use this information as a starting point.

It is critically important to keep a spirit of openness and investigation when trying to understand the Cayce readings and the human body. For example, it is easy to think "Now I know what the readings mean when they talk about the 'superficial or deep circulation,'" only to find that the next reading or a deeper understanding of physiology and anatomy gives a different picture. For example, massage along the spine with a "circular motion" to directly stimulate the sympathetic chain on the other side of the osseous spinal wall, and thereby certainly increasing coordination of neurological systems, is a technique worth pursuing, but exactly how this actually works is not yet clear. An open mind and an investigative spirit are necessary if we are to truly understand Cayce's healing concepts.

The readings' source often described the desired procedure in a few words, but frequently sent the supplicant to professionals such as Drs. Reilly, Dobbins or others because their knowledge and procedures were so appropriate that no description was deemed necessary. We don't have Cayce, Reilly or Dobbins, so we must do the best we can. This makes it doubly important not to become locked into rigid, preconceived notions of a therapeutic technique. The readings consistently support our reliance on inner awareness. We must couple this with discrimination and intelligent, carefully learned skill.

I don't agree with some of Joe and Sandra's conclusions and procedures. My experience is different. But this is their experience and they are presenting it to us as another tool toward our growing understanding of healing and health. You too must think and draw your own conclusions. Keep your brain in gear and your heart open.

A note of caution. Seek the advice of a licensed physician if you, as a patient, have any condition, or as a therapist, see any condition which may be a contraindication to any of the treatments suggested in this book. Some examples are heart or circulatory problems which may be made worse by increased body temperature in a "cabinet sweat" or similar procedure. Other examples are varicosities or thrombophlebitis where inappropriate massage could cause a blood clot to be released into the circulation. Remember, internal use of Atomidine should only be by prescription of a physician. Finally, remember that all treatments are not necessarily good for everybody. When seeking to aid, remember that each person is unique and that most of the readings were given for individuals.

Students of the Edgar Cayce readings and those who knew Dr. Harold Reilly may well ask how a book about Cayce and massage could be written without a large section on Dr. Reilly's contribution. The short answer is that it is so complex it requires a separate book by someone who worked extensively with him. You will not find very much specific information about Dr. Reilly's methods in the readings because when the readings recommended him, they left it to Dr. Reilly as to how to give the massage. Also, in these specific readings and in Reilly's practice, massage was rarely used alone. In his book, *The Edgar Cayce Handbook for Health Through Drugless Therapy*, massage receives two of fifteen chapters.

So, with the above proviso, it is entirely appropriate for this book not to focus on Dr. Reilly; that subject requires its own book. The Duggans' book stands on its own merits, as the result of two people seeking answers. As such, it gives us a new window into previously unexplored comments from the readings about massage, and much food for thought. We owe a debt of gratitude to Joe and Sandra for their exploration and writing. Enjoy the book. It is an excellent contribution to understanding what the Edgar Cayce readings say about massage. We may never know the whole story. But isn't that what makes the search interesting?

James Arnold Baker, D.C.
Research Coordinator
National College of Chiropractic

PREFACE

The Edgar Cayce Readings &
A Brief History of Massage

Recommendations for massage in the Edgar Cayce health readings are deeply rooted in the history of massage from the 1850s to the 1950s. Edgar Cayce (1877 – 1945) was a medical clairvoyant for forty-three years, providing medical diagnoses and treatment suggestions for thousands of people needing help. His psychic source drew on a vast knowledge of herbs, hydrotherapies, medicines, massage, mechanical and electrical devices, osteopathy and much more. The information in the readings was given for specific individuals and varied with each one, although one could say that the types of treatments such as osteopathy, massage, and hydrotherapy were the most frequently offered.

Transcripts of Cayce's readings, records, reports, and affadavits by patients and doctors are all on file at the Association for Research and Enlightenment in Virginia Beach, Virginia. Patients' names have been replaced with numbers to perserve privacy. For example, 2387 would be the reading number for a specific person. 2387-2 would be that same person's second reading, 2387-5 their fifth reading, and so on. There are almost 9,000 health readings, about 75% of these containing recommendations for massage as part of the treatment plan.

Today in the late 1980s it's often difficult to imagine that less than 100 years ago massage was used for many medical conditions, among them: anemia, apoplexy, neuritis, neurasthenia, laryngitis, bronchitis, colds, heart diseases, constipation, diabetes, sprains, rheumatism, arthritis, scleroderma, fractures, polio, cerebral palsy, multiple sclerosis, muscular dystrophy, diseases of the digestive organs, and many more. But it's true. In fact, many of the most prominent physicians and surgeons of the 19th and early 20th centuries recommended, practiced, and wrote about the successful use of massage for both medical conditions and the musculoskeletal system.

For example, John Harvey Kellogg, M.D., a surgeon, wrote hundreds of articles and books, some of which were devoted to massage and hydrotherapy. In 1895 he published *The Art of Massage: Its Physiological Effects and Therapeutic Applications*. In 1884 Douglas Graham, M.D., wrote *Massage: Manual Treatment and Remedial Movements*. By 1913 there was a fourth edition, including over 1400 medical case studies on massage. Graham was also a prolific writer of articles for medical journals. Today these works are neglected by the medical community in favor of more complex therapies using pharmaceuticals and more of a mechanical, electrical, or electronic nature, such as ultrasound.

Ironically, one of the great contributions to soft tissue massage was by James H. Cyriax, M.D., a British orthopedic surgeon. In 1941 he published *Massage, Manipulation and Local Anesthesia*, a book about deep massage. However, the medical world tended to apply his injection techniques rather than massage in keeping with their increasing orientation to and use of modern pharmacologies. Within twenty years, deep tissue massage had moved away from the medical community and become part of conventional massage as it became increasingly more popular in the second half of the 20th century.

As massage became more neglected from the 1920s to the late 1950s, this same approximate period saw its continued widespread use in the Edgar Cayce health readings which emphasized natural means of healing and drugless therapies such as diet, rest, exercise, hydrotherapies, packs, herbs, osteopathy, chiropractic, and massage.

It's important to understand the scope of massage therapy in the Edgar Cayce psychic readings. Here are thousands of diagnoses (we might well call them case studies) given between 1910 and 1945 for all kinds of ailments with some type of massage as part of the treatment plan in about 75% of them. These readings include almost every known type of massage available in America in that period – Swedish Massage; osteopathic massage; general massage; local massage (e.g., abdominal massage or massage to the joints only); neuropathic massage; vibratory massage; spinal massage, and deep massage.

During the last twenty years, there has been a renewed interest in massage all across the country. This is related to our increasing awareness and understanding of health as an ongoing process involving body, mind, environment, and spirit. We are learning how to be responsible for our own health and how to maintain more equilibrium, balance, cooperation, and coordination in our lives day by day. We are learning how our mind, emotions, and attitudes have profound effects on our nervous system, which in turn affects our entire body. Today massage has increasingly come into its own as a therapy uniquely suited to helping people feel better physically *and* emotionally.

Massage in the Edgar Cayce readings may have been part of treatments for specific ailments with emphasis on traditional physiological effects on venous and lymph circulation, the skin, the nervous systems, and muscles, but it was also used to coordinate different body systems, such as the superficial with the deep circulation, the eliminations with assimilation, and the cerebrospinal and sympathetic nervous systems. Cayce also gave information describing the relationship between the soul, mind, and body based on the balance of the sympathetic system. He said, "The activity of the mental or soul force of the body may control entirely the whole physical through the action of the balance in the sympathetic system" (Edgar Cayce, 5717-3).

This book focuses on massage, specifically on spinal massage and how it helps balance the sympathetic nervous system. The concepts and the techniques provide a new dimension in both the history and current practice of massage. And it adds to our understanding of healing as a process of coordination, cooperation, and integration of body, mind, and spirit.

INTRODUCTION

I decided to learn massage when I was forty-seven years old. It was what is popularly called a "mid-life career change." For twenty years I had been a teacher and sculptor and for the last four years had been struggling to overcome a lymphoma type cancer. At the time, I used chemotherapy as the main mode of therapy because this was all I knew. Fortunately, I also began reading Zen literature, something that had always interested me. This led to daily sessions of meditation and strange experiences of light. I also began experiments with breathing and concentration. Looking back on all this now from the vantage point of a great deal more reading and experience, it is obvious that my survival was a "healing," a healing which was the result of practices I little understood.

My wife Sandra and I were now living with our daughter in Virginia Beach, Virginia. Sandra was the Supervisor of the A.R.E. Therapy Department. For reasons little understood by me, I too was gradually becoming interested in healing. I learned that Dr. Harold J. Reilly would be in Virginia Beach within a few days. Fortunately, I was able to meet with him, and what a memorable experience it was. He was 87 years old then and going strong. We got along well with each other and he agreed to teach me his long-famous method of massage.

It would be another six months before Dr. Reilly returned to Virginia Beach, but this allowed me time to think and prepare. I decided to take lessons from one of Dr. Reilly's students. This would give me a chance to evaluate my desire, ability, and attitudes with regard to massage.

I enjoyed learning massage and giving it over the next six months. I practiced on anyone who wanted a free massage and I never lacked for volunteers. It was a year later that I received a second Reilly massage that differed so much from what I had been taught that I knew I needed to be taught by Dr. Reilly himself.

Sandra and I dreamed now of returning to our home in Connecticut and opening a business in massage and hydrotherapy. I had received personal instruction from Dr. Reilly, but realized almost immediately that ten hours of instruction for the purpose of relaxation only would not be sufficient for a professional practice where health problems would be encountered. The massage described in his book, *The Edgar Cayce Handbook for Health Through Drugless Therapy,* is under the heading "Instructions For Home Massage," and it is substantially the very same massage he taught me to give. Clearly it was a good massage for relaxation, the practitioner being taught to massage "*upward* and *toward* the heart," using light to hard pressure, and a slow tempo for relaxation. The technique of instruction was to use basic massage strokes on an anatomical part as a whole (e.g., the upper leg is treated as a unit).

This massage may have been adequate for the A.R.E. Therapy Department, where only a relaxing, caring massage was expected, but it clearly wouldn't suffice for a professional practice. At that time, I thought I could prepare myself for future self-employment by researching the Edgar Cayce readings on health, for it is common knowledge among many members of the A.R.E. that massage is one of the most frequently recommended therapies in the 8,968 physical health readings, maybe even the most recommended. Added to this was the legendary name given to the massage taught by Dr. Reilly, *The Cayce-Reilly Massage.*

We decided to move back to Connecticut within five months. That surely should be enough time to get valuable information from the readings on massage. Needless to say, I found very little because the practice, techniques, and theories of massage were not indexed as such. The major entry for massage is under "Physiotherapy: Massage: Oils," almost 6,700 references! In lieu of this, I could look under subjects such as paralysis, scoliosis, arthritis, etc., hoping to discover something about massage. Consequently, at the end of five months, I had very little information.

During this period we learned another technique of massage called "deep muscle therapy." Again the massage was taught by anatomical parts rather than by muscle groups. It was much more complicated than Reilly's massage, using basic cross-fiber techniques. Its purpose was to help chronically contracted muscles regain improved tone and function. We felt a little more comfortable opening a business with this additional skill.

Looking ahead to future licensing requirements for the practice of massage therapy, (licensing was already required in some states), we graduated from the Stillpoint Center School of Massage in Amherst, MA and joined a professional organization for massage therapists – the A.M.T.A. (American Massage Therapists Association). With diplomas in hand, membership in the A.M.T.A., Sandra's nursing license and having attended many workshops in deep muscle therapy, polarity therapy, and so on, we offered a service in massage and hydrotherapy.

For four years we maintained quite a successful practice in Connecticut, located across from a small town hospital. Much to our surprise and delight we found people were receptive and open to massage. One wonderful elderly lady said she had always wanted a "real massage" and was just waiting for the right place to come along.

Working together was exciting, fun and rewarding. We could easily consult with each other and discuss problems our clients were having; two heads were better than one. One day we literally worked together on a ten-year-old boy to shorten the massage because his mother felt his patience and attention span were low. He loved it, fell asleep and couldn't wait to come again!

We also continued to study, learn and grow in our knowledge of holistic health. We began teaching massage workshops with the focus on family members and friends helping each other. Cayce had often said that the daily spinal massages were to be given by those closest to the person requesting the reading. A loving, caring attitude was as valuable as the spinal massage patterns.

Unfortunately, I became seriously ill with a kidney infection and was unable to work for two months. Within another month, I had an automobile accident. Unable to work for another two and a half months, we were just about out of business. We decided to return to Virginia Beach where the warm air and warm salt water would help me heal. We applied for work in the A.R.E. Therapy Department and were offered positions. Also, a teaching position was available for me in the newly forming Harold J. Reilly School of Massotherapy.

Once back in Virginia Beach I again began doing research on massage. For years I had been aware of how difficult it is for people to research the subject in the Edgar Cayce readings. Most of us are overwhelmed with the catalogue's references to massage. In many cases, the word *massage* is followed by the specific name of an oil, such as myrrh, tincture of benzoin, pine oil, or peanut oil. As we look down the long file of cards – remember, there are over 6,700 references in this section – frustration looms its head. As I said earlier, I could go to a specific health problem in the Index to find information on massage. But what I was looking for was material on how to give a massage from the point of view of a massage *therapist*. (In the readings and up until about the 1970s, the words *masseur* and *masseuse* were used. The preferred description by persons with professional training is *massage therapist*.) This type of information was hard to find in any systematic way, and there wasn't anyone who could help me. Invariably, I received the same reply when asking for assistance. There were just too many references to too many oils – as if somehow the oils were the heart of the massage.

Next, I turned to Dr. Harold J. Reilly's book[1] and his section on massage. Here was a brief history of massage and personal stories of his work with both clients in New York and persons with readings from Edgar Cayce. They were all success stories and very interesting, but not much on the practice of massage. Then Dr. Reilly gave instructions for the "Reilly Method of Home Massage." He gave no history of his technique or its relationship to the Edgar Cayce readings. But he did begin the instruction by saying: "While I would not attempt to compare the benefit of home massage to that given by a *competent operator*, you will be surprised at how much benefit you can derive from mastering some simple techniques" (Reilly, p. 258). In other words, there was a lot more to learn if you wanted to practice massage *professionally.*

Next, I looked at Dr. McGarey's book, *The Edgar Cayce Remedies,* and the section on massage. He said, "The Cayce readings dealt with specifics many times, for many people, but apparently never gave a routine that might be followed for the average person in need of a general massage." So Dr. McGarey gave directions for a massage, "The A-B-C's of Massage." The purpose of massage, he said, was "relaxation, lymphatic cleansing, and balancing of the nervous systems." [2]

As I look back, comparison of Reilly's "Home Massage," the massage he taught me when I trained with him, and "The A-B-C's of Massage" left me with three different methods and little understanding as to why they differed. However, I was aware of many similarities between these massages and Swedish Massage. (This point will be discussed later.) For now, I had been in the library for several weeks and was getting nowhere. But Dr. McGarey's saying "balancing of the nervous system" as an aim of massage intrigued me because I didn't know what that meant.

I began to look through the Index under *nervous system.* The largest number of cards was under the heading, *Nervous Systems: Incoordination,* a whole tray with over 1,000 cards, all blank, other than the heading and a reading number, and all looking pristine – never touched, thumbed, or used! Using a scatter technique, I wrote down approximately 15-20 reading numbers at random from the beginning, middle and end of the section.

I was overwhelmed. The first nine out of ten readings all had massage as a therapy plus at least six to seven different types of massage, some of which I knew nothing about. There was osteopathic massage, neuropathic massage, Swedish massage, a "good" massage, "massage," and various types of spinal massage. Sometimes the spinal massage moved from the 9th dorsal down and up and out to the extremities, or from the extremities in to the 9th dorsal, or from the base of the brain to the base of the spine. There were specific instructions for circular massage of the cerebrospinal system and the sympathetic nervous system.

I added another 20 reading numbers and continued the search. Once in a while, I branched out to *Eliminations: Incoordination* or *Circulation: Lymph: Incoordination* and discovered techniques for abdominal massage, lymphatic massage, lymphatic pumps, or rubdowns.

The sheer volume of information was too hard to control without a system to organize it. I went to Mae St. Clair in the Readings Research Department at A.R.E. and shared with her what I was finding. (She had worked directly with the late Edgar Cayce.) She encouraged me and showed me a method she used when doing research. Also, it turned out that we both had come to similar findings regarding the significance of the nervous system and coordination or incoordination in the Cayce health readings, for it was within this indexing that I was discovering so much about massage. Mae suggested I count all the cards which might relate to the research I was undertaking.

First, a word about the 6,700 references to oils used with massage. Many readings called for formulas with three, four and five oils in combination. Using three as a conservative figure, this would indicate there are approximately 2,200 readings in which massage is recommended with specific oils. These oils were suggested for their healing properties. Yet, there are many readings where no oil was recommended, either because the massage didn't require oil, such as osteopathic or neuropathic massage, or the specific healing dimensions of an oil were not needed for a particular individual.

Next, it is important to know about a reading given on February 24, 1937, concerning the significance of massage and osteopathy in the readings as a whole. I didn't come across this reading until after many months of research, but I feel it needs to be spoken about here so that the chart's significance will be clear. In Cayce reading 1158-11, the following information is given concerning coordination and what treatment best brings this about.

For as understood by the body, and by the one that would make the mechanical or osteopathic adjustments, *or the massage or masseuse* activity, there is every force in the body to recreate its own self – if the various portions of the system are coordinating and cooperating one with another.

Hence the reason why, *as we have so oft given from the sources here*, that mechanical adjustments as may be administered by a thorough or serious osteopathic manipulator may nearer adjust the system for its perfect unison of activity than most any other means – save under acute or specific conditions; and even then the more oft such become necessary. (Edgar Cayce, 1158-11, p. 3, my italics)

This means that osteopathy was the most frequently given treatment in the physical readings because it helped – more than any other method – the body to coordinate one part with another to achieve a unity of activity.

The total number of health readings is said to be 8,968. If osteopathy was the most frequently chosen therapy, then the 4,500 references to it indicate that it was 50% of the total. It is hard to get a count on massage, but it was probably almost equal to osteopathy based on what was said in reading 1158-11. No other therapies come close to these figures. Here is a sample.

Therapy	Number of Readings	% of Health Readings
Electric Vibrator	400	4%
Wet Cell Appliance	1,000	11%
Radio-Active Appliance	1,000	11%
Infra-Red Heat	150	2%
Chiropractic	450	5%
Oils	2,500	27%

Then I set up another small chart in relation to the nervous systems. I wanted to find out how many readings or references were made to the nervous system compared to the lymph, eliminative, digestive systems and the glands.

Topic	Number of Readings
Nervous System	1,700
Neuralgia	400
Neurasthenia	400
Neuritis	400
Spine (includes spinal subluxations)	1,500
Subtotal of the above Nerve related readings	4,075
Lymph	450
Assimilation:	
Elimination: Incoordination	600
Elimination: Incoordination	700
Glands	2,000

Interpreting figures like these is a risky business, but if we're just looking for a general configuration of some kind and take into account that any one reading may have 40 indexed references to it (e.g., a formula for an oil containing five different substances would be indexed five times; a card for each substance), some generalizations can be drawn. Allowing for duplication in the above chart under *Nervous Systems*, especially in reference to spinal subluxations which usually also appear under *Nervous Systems: Incoordination*, the total comes to 3,075 or 34% of the total health readings. *Functions* comes to 20% and *glands* to 22%. So incoordination of the nervous systems represents a significant percentage of the health readings.

These figures led me to a more intensive study of massage as related to the nervous systems. At first I was a little intimidated by the anatomy and the physiology of the readings and the references to various types of massage, such as neuropathic massage, osteopathic massage, *good* massage. But then I discovered a letter from Edgar Cayce to a young man who had been receiving readings for epilepsy. Apparently, he wanted quick results and was willing to do almost anything; in this case, he wanted to use hypnotism before receiving the treatments from a naprapath recommended in the first reading. When Cayce found out his intentions from the parents, he wired the son not to undergo hypnotism until after the other treatments. Then in a longer letter to the young man, Cayce analyzed the reading, giving his interpretation as to why hypnotism wasn't advisable yet. In so doing, he said: "I am not a physician, but unless this information in the readings is *plain common sense* we can't make it very practical" (E.C., 567-2, p. 7, my italics).

What did Edgar Cayce mean by "plain common sense"? I believe he meant that the physical readings were not something to be decoded. The anatomy and physiology were known simple facts about the location of body parts, how they function, and especially how they function together or in coordination. He expected the person either to know this or be able to find out for himself. A reading might give information about the heart, lungs, liver, and kidneys; the processes of elimination and digestion; the function of the lymph system and a little about the nervous systems. When, however, his sources differed from conventional anatomy and physiology, the readings often gave a detailed account of its viewpoint. All this points to Cayce's belief (conscious and unconscious) that everyone can and should know their bodies and how to maintain them. Health and healing is not the sole responsibility of professionals, and the knowledge is not mysterious but "plain common sense."

I also researched the history of massage, especially the period from about the 1850s to the 1940s – the latter years being simultaneous with the period of the Cayce readings. I found out that there wasn't anything new about the massage techniques in the Cayce readings – they were, in fact, well known at the turn of the century. When Cayce called for a professional massage, it was specified as Swedish, osteopathic, neuropathic, or the "general" massage, or to be done by a masseuse or masseur. If a friend or family member could do it, that was so stated. But when specific directions were given – especially circular massage along the cerebrospinal and sympathetic nervous systems in a specific direction – I knew Cayce was looking at massage from a different perceptual field. It was not so much that the technique was different, but the purpose; he was adding another dimension to the mechanical aspects. So, over and over again, I was reading about the coordination of the cerebrospinal with the sympathetic nervous system, or the sympathetic nervous system with the lymph system or the eliminations, etc.

Thus, in order to understand why a particular massage was recommended, it is important to first understand the concept of coordination in the physical readings and then the concept of how the nervous systems function within the body. Next, specific massage techniques must be studied within the context they were given. Finally, hydrotherapy and healing oils are so much a part of the Cayce approach that we need to study them in order to fully comprehend the Edgar Cayce vision of massage in health maintenance and healing.

Throughout our years as massage therapists, our hopes, dreams, and goals were to help others learn to help themselves by using the Cayce principles of holistic health. We wanted to share our experiences of discovering that health is a state of balance that needs ongoing maintenance and T.L.C. (tender loving care) on all three levels – spiritual, mental, emotional and physical. Massage and hydrotherapy, with their ancient roots in healing, seemed to be the right way to do this. Learning to reach out and touch each other would help dispel the alienation, despair and loneliness that so many are feeling in today's world.

Endnotes:

[1] Harold J. Reilly, D.Ph.T., D.S. and Ruth Hagy Brod. *The Edgar Cayce Handbook for Health Through Drugless Therapy.* (Virginia Beach, VA: A.R.E. Press, 1987) newest edition.

[2] William A. McGarey, M.D. *The Edgar Cayce Remedies.* (New York: Bantam, 1983).

Edgar Cayce's
MASSAGE
Hydrotherapy
& Healing Oils

Chapter One

THE MIND & MASSAGE

The simple truth is, happy people generally don't get sick. One's attitude toward oneself is the single most important factor in healing or staying well. Those who are at peace with themselves and their immediate surroundings have far fewer serious illnesses than those who are not.
— Bernie Siegel, *Love, Medicines and Miracles*

Last winter I was driving along an icy road in a rural area of Connecticut. I was thinking about a future workshop planned for another part of the country, especially because it would take me to a warmer climate. My mind wandered to appointments I had within the next few hours, to thinking of where I had just been and feeling good about it. Suddenly, the car was skidding on the ice and my attention reverted to the road and the car, but it was too late! The car went out of control and crashed into a utility pole. I ended up in the hospital with a broken leg and concussion.

This simple, but tragic, sequence of events is a good example of how one's consciousness can affect the physical body. An automobile has no brain, but it does have an engine to make it go. The brain is provided by the driver; the car, in effect, becomes an extension of that driver. Direction and speed of the car are provided by the driver's hands on the steering wheel, foot on the gas pedal and conscious awareness of road conditions and speed limits. Need I say, failure to live in the present while driving a car over icy roads often leads to disaster, as it did for me. My brain wasn't paying attention to the road signals; it was daydreaming about the past and the future. The cortex had given up direct control of the car and, therefore, the foot on the gas pedal couldn't respond to changes in road conditions. You *have* to stay in the present – the NOW – as all spiritual teachers teach. Anger, resentment, happy or unhappy memories and thoughts of the past, expectations, worries, and fears of the future only separate you from what is right in front of you – all those signals, sounds, clues, to a living present.

Commonly in stressful situations like this (and in the expression of strong emotions like anger and fear), once we become conscious or aware of what we are doing, we find we are out of control. It's too late for our brain to respond and change the physiological response (change the speed and direction of the car, or overcome our anger, etc.).

According to Dr. Phil Nuernberger, author of *Freedom from Stress*, "the reason we suffer from stress is because we are insensitive to the mental and physical habits and patterns which maintain a constant level of activation in our bodies and minds" (p.97). He says we are not paying attention to our thoughts or emotions; we aren't aware of what our nervous system is doing or how it is affecting our body. Only when we get into an accident or a divorce or a critical illness – in other words, overwhelmed – do we become aware of our feelings and emotions. If we can learn how to become sensitive or conscious of our emotional pressures before we get into overwhelming or disastrous situations, we have a better opportunity for controlling or changing them and lessening their effects.

To help understand this process, let's look a little closer at how the brain works, expecially the relationship between the brain and physiological responses. Inside the brain, the hypothalamus (see illustration 1) is responsible for maintaining equilibrium in the body at an unconscious level. It responds to hot, cold, thirst, hunger, and knows how to respond to emotions like anger and fear. The hypothalamus, in turn, controls the pituitary gland, the gland known as the "master gland" – the controller of the endocrine system. At a higher level, the limbic system or the so-called "emotional brain" controls the hypothalamus. The limbic part of the brain responds to fear, anger, resentment, love, jealousy, joy – in short, our emotions and feelings. These are transmitted to two areas very near the hypothalamus. One area connects to the sympathetic nervous system and the other to the parasympathetic. Together they are referred to as the *autonomic nervous system.* Its function is to control the visceral functions of the body (i.e., organs in the body cavity), mostly at an unconscious level.

At the next highest level, the cortex has learned to control the hypothalamus from information received either externally, from the environment, or internally, from the body. For example, by consciously monitoring visual signals of the road, we keep our cars from hitting poles and other cars by continually sending nerve impulses from our eyes directly and voluntarily down the spinal cord and out to muscles which control the gas pedal and steering wheel.

We are also aware of an even higher level where wishes, decisions, and imagination can control the cortex. It is here that visualization, meditation, and attitude can intervene and help change our unconscious physiological responses. For many of us, unfortunately, our lives have included accidents, life-threatening illnesses, difficult relationships and so on. Knowing a little of how the brain functions helps us to understand these connections between our mind and body, and to regain and maintain health, balance and harmony.

The work of Carl and Stephanie Simonton described in their book, *Getting Well Again*, is a good example of how our awareness can be increased through understanding. They teach that "we all participate in our own health through our beliefs, our feelings, and our attitudes toward life, as well as in more direct ways, such as through exercise or diet" (p. 3). Their work is based on using relaxation and mental imagery techniques with conventional medical treatments.

The Simonton's first patient, a 61-year-old man with throat cancer and a 5% chance of living more than five years, proved to be a dramatic example of the success of their theories of healing. Using primarily relaxation and mental imagery, the results were outstanding.

Dr. Simonton explained to the man how he himself "could influence the course of his own disease" (p. 7). The program was described and within two months of practicing relaxation and visualization three to five times a day, the man showed no sign of the cancer. Feeling elated about his ability to control the whole process, he decided to work with his arthritis. Because of his success with alleviating this condition, he decided to apply the techniques to his impotence – a problem for more than twenty years. Again he applied visualization and within weeks resumed full sexual activity.

In *Love, Medicine and Miracles*,   Dr. Bernie Siegel describes research on what is called "psychosocial dwarfism." This condition is a result of the pituitary gland's failure to produce sufficient hormones. When a young child lives in a family situation of hostility and rejection, the child's self-esteem suffers; he may feel unloved and unworthy. His limbic brain functions by telling the hypothalamus to respond to this lack of self-worth which in turn signals the pituitary gland to suppress its production of growth hormones.

In the Cayce readings (covering a period roughly from 1920 – 1944), the idea of the body, emotions, mind, "imaginative forces," and spirit working together as a whole was totally accepted. Work in biofeedback by Elmer and Alyce Green was just beginning to be published around 1970. The work of people like the Simontons and Siegel didn't appear until 1978 and 1986, respectively. In 1970, before the above research had been done, Dr. Wm. McGarey, Director of the A.R.E. Clinic in Phoenix, expressed his hope that Cayce's mind-body connection would come to be recognized. "Perhaps we will gradually accept more and more the fact that emotions cause physical changes through glandular outpourings of hormones and increased flow of energies especially over the sympathetic nervous system."[1]

For example, in a reading for a 51-year-old woman school teacher suffering from asthenia, a loss of strength and energy, Cayce gave a single treatment program: gentle massage, some osteopathic adjustments and dietary advice. He traced the cause of her asthenia to anxiety and tension directly affecting the nervous system:

Also, there has been, and exists in the present, incoordination between the nerve systems of the body. An over-anxiety, a fear has caused overtension in the nervous system, especially as related to the areas in the upper dorsal or through the brachial centers, and has caused a great shock to the body, so that the ability of the nerves to coordinate in replenishing energies through the circulation has caused this great weakness which exists in the body.

These may be materially aided but it will require as much activity of the mental self as those administrations from any mechanical or medicinal natures. (Edgar Cayce, 5240-1)

One can infer from the mention of mental discipline as being just as important as the physical treatments that her difficulties weren't going to be easily resolved.

In a letter to A.R.E. seven years after her reading (1951), she explained the source of the shock, blaming the principal of her school:

The shock was an emotional upset, partly caused by a half-crazed principal with whom I was unfortunatley working after my thyroidectomy when I was weak. In his mental weakness (he had suffered severe mental trouble and I had of necessity filled his office), he had the idea I wanted his position and was more then unjust and cruel. Other than that, I do not care to discuss the problem. I learned that a shock to a weak physical body can be very damaging. (Edgar Cayce, 5240-1)

However one interprets the "emotional upset," it remains an example of the mind and spirit affecting the nervous system.

In a reading for a 34-year-old woman suffering from Hodgkin's disease, Cayce traced the cause to an injury to the 6th and 7th dorsal sustained four years previous to the reading. He called the resulting effect a lymphitis (inflammation of the lymphatics). The reaction to this was excess fluid in the feet, knees, hips, abdomen, lungs, face and neck.

She followed Cayce's plan for treatment and got well within three months. But five years later, "she had much emotional trouble with her husband and the physical condition came back on her."[2] She separated from her husband and died at the age of 39!

That is a dramatic example of how one's emotions affect

one's life for better or worse. Our desire to live, to have meaningful relationships, to be loved and to love others all affect our health and ultimately whether we live or die.

What does all of this have to do with massage? Massage might be looked at as one kind of biofeedback information. Elmer and Alyce Green of the Menninger Foundation in Topeka, Kansas, write:

Biofeedback per se is merely the feedback to a person of some of his or her own biological information, usually by means of a visual indicator, or by a tone. The specific sensory mode of feedback, usually vision or hearing, can on occasion have an effect on the rate of learning, but the important feature in biofeedback training is not the sensory mode, but the content, the *information* which is fed back. And that information must reach the cortex and be understood in order for *self*-regulation to occur in the autonomic nervous system.[3]

The sensory information from massage comes through nerve receptors in the skin and muscles (the effect on veins and lymphatic vessels is mechanical). If the massage is perceived as gentle, loving and caring, the limbic system sends this message to the hypothalamus which sets a tone for relaxation and rebalance and healing. On the other hand, if the massage or touch is too deep, painful, or erratic, an opposite response may be set off and the body becomes alert. If the person is unable to allow a gentle, relaxing massage to penetrate into the limbic system, his or her body will remain in the same physiological condition.

The Greens also point out that biofeedback is more than just using some kind of visual or tactile feedback machine to train the body. Its more important function is to teach people how to listen to their own body so adjustments can then be made to control their minds, emotions, and bodies. Even more significant is its possibilities for transformation: "At any level of existence (physical, mental, emotional, spiritual) transformation may be usefully defined as a self-induced (autogenic[4]) movement toward greater health – physical, emotional, mental, or spiritual."[5]

There is a very interesting case in the Cayce readings of a young woman who "had been practically an invalid (mentally) for a number of years,"[6] and was considered a hopeless case medically. She had been hospitalized for four years. Background information in a Cayce letter stated:

The lady had been under the care of some physicians associated with John Hopkins for several months; they considered the case quite hopeless, in fact told her husband that nothing could be done – she might be better, she might be worse – and advised him to travel with her as long as his money lasted, then leave her somewhere. (Edgar Cayce, 4125-6)

Further, according to Cayce, the husband told him, "he didn't know whether it was best to let her go in the ocean or to give her an overdose of the medicine" (Edgar Cayce, 272-3). Imagine!

The first reading described her symptoms: shortness of breath, rapid pulse, severe headaches, clamminess in her legs and lower torso, and a general feeling of loss of self-control.

Cayce's reading identified the originial source of the problem as both physical and mental. The first reading identified surgery as the external condition that "brought about the shocks to the nervous system" (E.C., 4125-1). A month later a specific question about an abortion was asked. "Did these conditions in the body accumulate years ago due to an abortion?" In reply, "These conditions are as the results of indiscretions sometime back in the activities of the body" (E.C., 4125-4). This introduces an internal cause related to choice and morality.

One can only wonder how this young woman felt over the years to have ended up as a hopeless medical case. Shock, fear, guilt and maybe nowhere to turn for support and understanding while pregnant and after the abortion, all left their imprint on her body and mind. While undergoing treatment recommended in the readings, she was continually advised to keep a positive, creative attitude toward herself and those around her and to remain only in a supportive, quiet, restful environment.

Keep as far away as possible from any discussions that cause dissensions, or from any influences that would hinder the body in following physically and mentally those suggestions given.

While there was little or no outward manifestation from the long strain physically which the body underwent, with the mental anticipations, with *realizations*, there came with the spoken word (where there were antagonistic expressions with the self, as indicated), combined with the strain on the physical and the imaginative (as outlined), those reactions that made for incoordination.

Now, quietness – and those stimuli by the corrective forces along the cerebro-spinal and sympathetic system, as given, will bring about the *continued* improvements. (E.C., 4125-6)

The actual treatment plan at first was very simple: gentle, relaxing massage, osteopathy, and a prescription for intestinal gas. The purpose of the massage was to relax "the system" so that the osteopathic adjustments would be effective. But much more is going on here because the massage, through the hands of the masseuse, had to convey a caring, loving and supportive attitude and be perceived as such by the woman if it were to be successful. Her condition necessitated that the environment of the massage would have to be pleasant and soothing to the sensory system rather than harsh or unpleasant; words spoken would have to be supportive and loving for they convey ideas, emotions, and feelings. Of course the *physiological* goal of the massage was to increase circulation and help elimination through the venous and lymph flow.

All of this is no small matter, for consider what Cayce said about the nervous system when asked how the woman's body was responding to the special electrical device (Radio-Active Appliance) being used.[7] He said she was responding properly; that is, the device was helping to coordinate the sympathetic and cerebrospinal nervous systems. Then he gave an astonishing discourse on these two systems. It is very important and deserves to be quoted in its entirety.

...Let's understand what the sympathetic and the cerebro-spinal nervous system *are* within the human body!

In the cerebro-spinal centers, here we have the brain, the spinal cord – which enters through all the cerebro-spinal system, passing through each vertebra, and the impingements on same often cause much of the distress to the body-physical. This may be represented as the *physical* organism.

There is lying along each side of the cerebro-spinal system a series, or on either side a cord known as the *sympathetic* nervous system. Not within the structural portions, but *connecting* with same at definite points....

The activities of these:

The cerebro-spinal, the nerve cord itself, acts for the physical attributes of the body through the *impulses*.

The sympathetic is the greater *impulsive* system.

Now, materially, very little is set up – in other than metaphysics – as to what is the functioning proper of the sympathetic system; but, as has been with this body, by destroying within the imaginative system much that had been builded morally and spiritually within self, became such a shock to the whole of the physical body as to produce – from the sympathetic system into the moral fibre of the cerebro-spinal system – those conditions that became as has been experienced by the body. Gradually, disassociation of ideas, disassociation of activities became active within the body, so that the body was racked by torments from without and from within; for there came no response either from the definite activity of the cerebro-spinal or the sympathetic system, and those centers that suffered were those that have been outlined as the ones needing – even yet – those stimuli occasionally that there may be kept coordination in the system.

Now, these have been released – these pressures, and there is gradually being created by the activities of the low electrical form that making for better associations and connections in the system; there is being gradually added by the activities of the thoughts of the body, by the activities in the glands that work both with the sympathetic and cerebro-spinal system, that which makes for better coordinating conditions.

Know that the moral fibre, that the spiritual activities of the system, are being set and attuned; or know that within self that set before self as its ideal. Hold fast then to that thou hast started building. We will find, not only will there be builded greater physical and mental abilities within the body, but to be able to give out more to others will be that mission in which the body will excel in many, many ways. (E.C., 4125-5)

Together, the pregnancy, the moral question it raised, the decision to have an abortion, hindsight about right and wrong, the surgery – all adversely affected the young woman physically, mentally, and spiritually: "Gradually, disassociation of ideas, disassociation of activities became active within the body, so that the body was racked by torments from without and from within" (E.C., 4125-5). And, interestingly, those areas which suffered most were "the cardiac plexus and secondary cardiac plexus," the heart center – that center of our being we associate with love and giving.

The adhesions that had developed as a result of the surgical abortion eventually were the cause of congestion and pressures in the sympathetic ganglia which led to her extreme distress.

The woman received her first reading on November 21, 1932. By the end of December, she was well and able to return to her home. Cayce himself was elated with the results and wrote a long letter (E.C., 272-3) to the Norfolk physician who helped the woman carry out the instructions in her readings.

She has responded most wonderfully; in fact, she has been able to return home and practically take up her life that had been all awry – and she away from her husband and son – for almost four years [hospitalized]. For this to be accomplished in, we might say, a few weeks – or a little more than two months – seems very remarkable. (Edgar Cayce, 4125-6; reports)

This isn't a reading overwhelmingly in support of massage, for it is just one of the treatments. However, for the massage therapist – for all of us – the case is invaluable in demonstrating how deeply our beliefs and decisions affect our very being at its deepest levels. All too often we carry these shocks and traumas in our physical body to the point of dysfunction, hospitalization, and critical illness. And not only does this affect ourselves, it affects our friends and family.

We cannot be expected to handle life's difficulties alone. For certain, it is almost impossible to recover from any type of illness alone. We need the loving support of others in treatment, in self-understanding and in the acquiring or regaining of self-love and self-respect.

Massage is one type of treatment – when appropriate – which helps one to relax and receive support from another's gentle and loving touch. It is a way of connecting with another soul.

Endnotes:

[1] William A. McGarey, M.D., *Edgar Cayce and the Palma Christi*, (Virginia Beach, VA: The Edgar Cayce Foundation, 1970) p. 48. See Appendix for complete book list.

[2] From a letter to Gladys Davis Turner, Edgar Cayce's life-long secretary.

[3] Greene, Elmer & Alyce, "Biofeedback & Transformation", *The American Theosophist* (May 1985) Vol. 72 No. 5 p. 142.

[4] Relaxation and mental imagery techniques.

[5] Greene, Elmer & Alyce, p. 145.

[6] Quoted from a personal letter of Edgar Cayce's relating to reading 4125.

[7] This is a device designed and recommended in the Cayce readings. See *The A.R.E. Journal* for related articles. A list of these articles, and others, is available through the A.R.E. Library, P.O. Box 595, Virginia Beach, VA 23451.

Chapter Two

A HOUSE OF CARDS

Art is the perfect marriage of psychic impulse and technical implementation.
- Jose A. Arguelles

I was a sculptor in the late 1960s and 1970s. Most of my work was welded steel. Welding steel is a fascinating process because it involves both destruction and creation at the same time. Using either acetylene or an electric arc, the welder heats and melts the steel parts to be joined at temperatures over 2300° F. and then adds a third rod of steel to fuse them all together in a weld. For a sculptor, the result is often a new form or a synthesis of ideas, feelings, and materials.

The use of steel and the techniques of welding often imply great strength, both in the process itself, because it requires handling heavy duty tools and materials, and in the resulting sculpture because welded joints allow heavy welds such as steel to be fused together in positions or managements which seemingly defy gravity. A cantilever construction is one example.

I also know that for the artist or sculptor, the whole act of creation is a meaningful experience that involves not only making but exploring – exploring the materials of one's environment and their possibilities and limitations and exploring one's self in terms of thought, creativity, imagination, fantasy, integrity, and intuition. It can be a journey along a path where there is much to be learned and even more to be experienced.

My work and attitude reached a turning point when I began to experience sculptures such as Richard Serra's "One-Ton Prop (House of Cards)" of 1969. It is made of four lead plates, each weighing 500 pounds and about 48" by 60." They are arranged like a cube with only their upper corners touching – reminiscent of a house of cards we've all made as kids. No welds, no bolts to hold the work together, only the delicate balance of the lead plates against each other, the floor, and gravity. This was an expression very different from that of sculpture welded, bolted, hinged, or nailed together. The "House" used other kinds of welds: tension, gravity, relationship, balance, coordination, cooperation. It also conveyed suggestions of child-like games and simplicity and the inevitable collapse or change at the slightest touch. Surely this was an expression of the nature of our very being: our dependence on others, the delicate balance in relationship, our existence within a material world, and our awareness of a non-material world of forces such as gravity and space and how they are created and recreated.

I remember, too, seeing a picture of one of Serra's works in a junk yard. How high could steel slabs be stacked until they fell? And what was the point of sculpture existing only in photographs?[1] Two points here. One refers to the integrity and balance any structure has by its own nature on this planet. The shape, weight, and number of slabs in relation to gravity and environment determine its own structure and when it will fall. Second, a photograph suggests that objects, like human beings, have a life of their own. They can't be frozen with welds or in a photograph or museum or anywhere else. Life is a moment-to-moment affair.

From this point of view, our actions and behavior become paramount in our experience of the world. In a kind of artist's workbook entry, Serra made a list beginning with verbs: to roll, to bend, to chip, to cut, etc.[2] These are transitive verbs describing a specific type of action or behavior to be performed on an object or piece of material when constructing a sculpture. They also describe what human beings do with their bodies or their neuromusculoskeletal system, as a physiologist might say.

In the practice of massage, it's easy to make up a similar list of transitive verbs: to stroke, to touch, to knead, to rub, to compress, to wring, to shake, to vibrate, to squeeze and to roll. Each verb describes what one person does to another during a massage. During this process, balance and coordination are essential both within the practitioner and in the process itself for the results to be effective.

Regardless of the process or behavior a person enters – sculpting, massaging, singing, meditating, building, and so on – signals or nerve impulses are sent to the autonomic nervous system from the spinal cord, the brain, and the hypothalamus. The autonomic nervous system transmits impulses to the body through two major subdivisions called the "sympathetic" and "parasympathetic" nervous systems (see illustration 6). The spinal cord and the brain are usually referred to together as the *cerebrospinal system* (or the *central nervous system*). The hypothalamus is influenced by the limbic system which is that part of our brain responsive to stress, feelings, and sensations, both internally and externally (see illustration 1). In turn, the hypothalamus plays a critical role in the control of the immune system and the endocrine glands.

In other words, for the body to become activated, there must first be impulses from the brain, impulses coming from our mind or state of consciousness as they interact with and respond to our internal and external environments and even our higher self or soul. Therefore, balance and coordination can be seen as a continuous process of integration among the body, mind and spirit.

This is what the Edgar Cayce readings on health emphasize. When balance and coordination exist on all three levels, both inwardly and outwardly, a healthy, harmonious condition prevails. When one part becomes out of balance or incoordinated either within itself or in relation to another part, a process of "dis-ease" begins. If not corrected, dis-ease can eventually lead to dysfunction and disease.

In the many thousands of readings given for individuals' health, over and over again Cayce describes the major causative factor of dis-ease as some kind of incoordination among or within body, mind and spirit. For example, there are incoordinations between attitude and physical development, between the stomach and other digestive organs, between the superficial and deep circulation, between one's work or life style and the body, and between the cerebrospinal and sympathetic nervous system (illustration 7).

In relation to spinal massage, the subject of this book, the most frequently mentioned incoordination is between the cerebrospinal and sympathetic nervous systems. One reading describes the cause of the person's condition as "the inability of the sympathetic and cerebrospinal [nervous systems] to coordinate properly with the general functioning of the system" (E.C., 4125-1). Another reading says: "As we find, the conditions are the effects or the results of disturbing conditions to the equilibrium of the body; to that which makes for the better coordination between the sympathetic or vegetative nerve forces and the cerebrospinal system" (E.C., 986-1). And to a professor of anatomy, Cayce says: "As we find, then, more of the involvement is in the nervous system, the energies of the body, the activities of the body having been such as to break down the proper coordination between the nervous systems; that is, the cerebrospinal *and* the sympathetic (or vegetative) systems, as indicated" (E.C., 3056-1).

Although it is difficult to be precise as to the exact nature of the incoordination between the nervous systems, it might be helpful to describe the general flow of nerve impulses to and from the spinal cord and brain, or central nervous system. Efferent nerve impulses, carrying information along motorneurons from the brain, pass down the spinal cord out through the dorsal roots to the spinal nerves which flow to the musculoskeletal system. Sensory receptors (or sensory memory) to touch, heat, cold, and so forth, send nerve impulses from the periphery of the body back to the brain via afferent nerve fibers which enter the spinal cord through the ventral roots.

Nerve fibers from motorneurons and sensory neurons flow together with sympathetic nerve fibers in both the spinal roots and spinal nerves. In a healthy, coordinated body, nerve impulses passing through spinal roots and spinal nerves should flow unimpeded. But being vulnerable to both physical and biological trauma, something often

39

happens to change or disrupt the flow in some way – injury, fever, bacteria, hormonal imbalance, etc. According to Cayce, this frequently results in an incoordination between the spinal cord (cerebrospinal or central nervous system) and the sympathetic nervous system. In other words, the disruption prevents the efficient flow of nerve impulses through the nerve fibers where they flow together between the cerebrospinal and sympathetic nervous systems.

After Cayce describes such conditions, suggestions are given for improvement. In the 8,968 readings on health, the most common suggestion for improvement, even with general health maintenance, is to, 1) regain coordination among various body systems and 2) improve eliminations of bodily waste and toxins. As I've said before, the most frequently recommended treatments are osteopathy and hydrotherapy (remember, Cayce includes massage in both of these treatments). In one reading regarding the need for improved eliminations, Cayce says that this "...is why osteopathy and hydrotherapy come nearer to being the basis of all needed treatments for physical disabilities" (E.C., 2545-5).

It is also clear that hydrotherapy treatments are recommended because they aid in relaxation, increased circulation *and eliminations*. The body, this wonderful house of cards, has four organs of elimination: the colon, kidneys, skin and lungs. Waste matter and toxins are carried to these areas by the blood and lymph fluid. If one or more organs are not working properly, the other organs have to carry an increased burden and the physical begins to experience feelings of dis-ease, such as headaches, joint aches, halitosis, etc.

Hydrotherapy treatments cleanse the body by increasing perspiration and elimination of wastes through these four organs. Therefore, it's important to understand that hydrotherapy in the readings almost always includes a bath, a cabinet sweat or fume bath, a colonic,[3] a rubdown, and an oil massage. For example, one reading says:

We would have the general hydrotherapy treatments; including, first, a general cabinet sweat, the sitz baths, the thorough rubdown and massage, with special reference in the massage to the lumbar and sacral axis. Also include the superficial activity over the limbs, the knees, the feet especially; also a coordinating with the deep massage – not so much adjustments as deep massage – to stimulate coordinating activity of the cerebrospinal and sympathetic nerve systems, as well as impulses of blood supply in these areas specifically. (E.C., 1772-2)

With close to 60% of the health readings recommending osteopathy and hydrotherapy as major types of treatment, and with massage alone or as part of a hydrotherapy treatment nearly equal in frequency to that of osteopathy, it is important to examine their common aspects. Namely, the ability to balance the cerebrospinal and sympathetic nervous systems and help bring the body into coordination.

When Cayce's "diagnosis" includes incoordination between the cerebrospinal and sympathetic nervous systems, spinal massage is one of the most frequently recommended types of massage. For example, "When the massage is given, it should be as a circular motion down either side of the spine" (E.C., 1553-16); or "We would massage along the cerebrospinal system equal parts of olive oil and tincture of myrrh, heating the oil to add the myrrh" (E.C., 372-8); and again:

Q-1. Where should the massage be given?
A-1. The massage should be rather on each side of the spine and on the spine itself, so that the centers, as in the 3rd cervical, 1st, 2nd, 3rd, and 4th dorsal, 9th dorsal and lumbar axis, where they connect between nerves of the sympathetic system and the cerebrospinal system, from the closer activities between these two systems. These we would do, then. (E.C., 1188-12)

And of great significance is this description of a spinal massage and how it affects the pair of sympathetic ganglionated cords on each side of the vertebral column.

Follow this with a gentle massage, that stimulates or relaxes by the stimulation of each of the ganglia along the cerebrospinal system; more specifically in the areas where the cerebrospinal and sympathetic coordinate – in the larger forms of the ganglia. These we find in the 1st, 2nd and 3rd cervical, 1st, 2nd and 3rd dorsal, 9th dorsal, and in the lumbar axis and coccyx center. (E.C., 3075-1)

In the same reading, one of the questions provides even more insight into the purpose and technique of spinal massage:

Q-7 Should the massage be osteopathic, or could it be given by someone other than an osteopath?

A-7 Anyone that understands the anatomical structure of the body, in knowing how to coordinate the sympathetic and cerebrospinal systems in the areas indicated. These are not merely to be punched or pressed, but the ganglia – while very small – are as networks in these various areas. Hence a gentle, circular massage is needed; using only at times structural portions as leverages, but not ever – of course – bruising structure. (E.C., 3075-1)

Although these examples are given out of context, their importance is in the similarity of treatment by massage – that is, spinal massage – and its ability to help coordinate the sympathetic and cerebrospinal nervous systems and stimulate sympathetic ganglia.

The concept of "keeping a balance – by the touch – between the sympathetic and the cerebrospinal system" is "real osteopathy," according to one of the Cayce readings (E.C., 1158-24). It is also a concept in spinal massage as noted in the passage from reading 3075-1 quoted in the previous paragraph.

This concept is also presented eloquently in the writings of Irvin M. Korr, Ph.D., DSC. Dr. Korr was the distinguished Professor of Physiology at Kirksville College of Osteopathic Medicine for thirty years (1945 to 1975) and subsequently Professor of Biomechanics at Michigan State University College of Osteopathic Medicine. He is now Professor of Medical Education at Texas College of Osteopathic Medicine.

Dr. Korr wrote a series of three articles about the role of the spinal cord in "organizing disease processes." One of the major concepts in these articles involves how the sympathetic nervous system functions to balance or coordinate the visceral functions of the body with its musculoskeletal activity. This has interesting parallels with the concept in the Cayce readings concerning incoordination between the cerebrospinal and sympathetic nervous systems. In addition, it provides one explanation for the emphasis on spinal massage and osteopathy as primary choices of treatment for incoordination in the nervous systems.

To understand Dr. Korr's theory, it's important to prepare ourselves to look at some time-honored views of the autonomic nervous system from a different perspective. We are used to medicine's major concerns with our insides – our organs or viscera. Osteopathic medicine, on the other hand, has traditionally placed its emphasis on the musculoskeletal system in keeping and restoring our health.

Dr. Korr points out that our lives are not the actions of our organs. "What *does* human life consist of?" asks Korr. "What does man do?" he replies. Man distinguishes himself by *doing* – he runs, works, plays golf, makes pictures, creates sculpture, builds buildings, massages people, sings, thinks, makes love and war. He writes, prays, meditates, practices medicine, teaches, and gives osteopathic manipulations. Thought, ideas, reason, attitudes, feelings, conceptualizing, intuition – all equally result in unique actions of some sort. And all have in common the use of the musculoskeletal system: muscles, tendons, ligaments, bones, joints. Man's "behavior is produced by muscles acting on joints." For Dr. Korr, "The musculoskeletal system is the primary machinery of life" and directed by the nervous system in a continuous response to both internal and external stimuli. Thus the whole system is referred to as the *neuromusculoskeletal system*.[4]

It is through the neuromusculoskeletal system that we act out our humanity and our individual personalities in the infinite variety of ways of being human.... Even the highest moral, ethical, philosophical, and religious principles have value only insofar as they lead to appropriate behavior.... Similarly, it is through our musculoskeletal systems that we act out and communicate our attitudes, fears, hopes, aspirations, beliefs, and childhood conditioning.[5]

The role of the rest of the body, according to Dr. Korr, is to support the musculoskeletal system. Care and maintenance of this system is a supportive function of the viscera or organs of the body which involves supplying fuel and building materials, removing waste products, defending against invasive properties, and repairing and regenerating tissue. The entire internal environment must be regulated so that the cells of the musculoskeletal system can carry out their work.

The skeletal muscles make up about 40% of our body and consume more energy than any other body tissues. Their demand for oxygen is enormous yet can vary in a matter of seconds. Consumption of raw materials is immense, as well as the production of metabolic wastes. Metabolism in muscles yields not only waste products but also a large amount of heat which has to be dissipated. This whole process presents an enormous problem logistically. The highly specialized processes of the viscera and heat exchange mechanisms must all work together smoothly for efficient functioning of the musculoskeletal system.

As fast as nutrients are assimilated, they must be replaced and the waste products eliminated. The blood plays a crucial role here as both supplier and remover of waste. At all times, a balance, or what is termed *homeostasis*, must be maintained.

Thus, there are two types of body systems always attempting to work supportively and cooperatively with each other. One involves body movement or the activities a person performs using muscles, bones and joints. These actions are many in number and occur in different environments. This is the musculoskeletal system. On the other hand, there is the viscera which must provide the necessary resources to the musculoskeletal system not only to keep them functioning, but also to prevent draining the body's resources in the process. There has to be a balance, a coordination – homeostasis.

Dr. Korr describes this moment-to-moment process of balancing as "tuning." He says, "Health requires that from moment to moment the visceral functions of the body must be continually attuned or adjusted to what the body as a whole is doing, how the person is acting at that moment with his neuromusculoskeletal system." As he points out, the implication of tuning is the "bringing into harmony" of many diverse parts and functions.

Without going into details which are explained fully in his article, I will just mention the most important functions he discusses. Blood chemistry must be maintained in terms of acid metabolite, oxygen and carbon dioxide. Blood flow needs to be controlled in relation to times of increased activity or rest. Heat loss and body temperature must be monitored, and kept at a minimum. In times of emergency or violent activity, body functions, such as digestion, peristalsis, secretions, and sphincter controls must be suppressed.

In conclusion, all these functions of the supportive machinery or viscera must be kept constantly in tune with the demands of the musculoskeletal system. "This is precisely," says Dr. Korr, "the function of the sympathetic nervous system as the mediator between the somatic [musculoskeletal system] and supportive [viscera] machinery of life."

And most importantly, the sympathetic nervous system as part of the autonomic system is always responding to impulses from the higher centers in the brain. Our state of consciousness – our ideas, imagination, plans, feelings, emotions, desires, thoughts, beliefs, creativity, and decisions ultimately result in a change of behavior which is related to musculoskeletal movement, as stated earlier.

In understanding the sympathetic nervous system as having a tuning or mediating function between the musculoskeletal system and the viscera of the body, we need to understand how the sympathetic differs from the parasympathetic nervous system. Together, the two are always referred to as the *autonomic nervous system* and are usually perceived as opposite branches of a system concerned with regulating body activity automatically or unconsciously. One is said to inhibit and the other to excite. All that is needed for good health is to balance the two systems.

The parasympathetic performs the housekeeping functions of the body when at rest and non-threatened. Digestion, eliminations, and decreased demands on the heart and circulation are characteristic of parasympathetic control. The sympathetic, on the other hand, is often referred to as the "fight or flight" system because it prepares the body to deal with stressful situations that will affect the body's homeostasis. Sympathetic conditions increase heart rate, blood pressure, blood sugar levels and dilate the bronchioles of the lungs and blood vessels in skeletal muscles. Blood is withdrawn from the digestive organs to support activities of the muscles, heart and brain.

Interestingly, the Cayce readings never use the terms _parasympathetic_ or _autonomic_. One assumption is that Cayce's use of "sympathetic" or "vegetative" for _autonomic_ included all of what is now called the autonomic nervous system because he did not see them functioning antagonistically. As Dr. McGarey says:

> The rather intricate functional makeup of the two parts of the autonomic nervous system tends to influence us to group them as separate entities, so to speak. We should probably hesitate, however, to do this simply because the source of the neurons is different and the function is apparently antagonistic. We note, for instance, that they are not really so antagonistic as one would think on first consideration. Rather they augment each other by their reciprocity. Perhaps like a good husband and wife working together.[6]

Dr. Korr, on the other hand, views them as two different systems; they have different functions in different areas. The parasympathetic is primarily "concerned with intuition, with replenishing body stores which are depleted under sympathetic direction."[7] The sympathetic system is mainly concerned with work, the use of muscular energy, and "it is concerned also in our mental and emotional attitudes toward that work and our responses to environmental forces."[8]

Even more striking are the differences that can be seen when a study of both systems also includes the somatic structures of the body. Only the sympathetic innervates (i.e., communicates nerve energy) both somatic and visceral tissues. The parasympathetic innervates only visceral parts of the body; nothing goes to the musculoskeletal system.

From this perspective, the sympathetic system assumes a strategic position between the brain, viscera, and somatic tissues. Impulses, imaginative tones, emotions – all from the brain or higher centers – affect the body primarily through the sympathetic nervous system. The significance of this in the Cayce readings is profound.

In a reading for a young man with hypertension, Cayce described the problem as an imbalance between development of "the spirit and soul sense" in relation to the physical body. "He subjugates it [soul and spirit] much by the action of the physical," says Cayce. The young man, like Cayce, had clairvoyant abilities but had difficulty expressing them. In an earlier life reading,[9] he had been given his life's purpose: "One whose greater force lies in the development of self toward the psychic forces as is reached through the position of Jupiter with Uranus" (E.C., 5717-1). But in the reading on his health, Cayce summed up the situation by saying that "the activity of the mental or soul force of the body may control entirely the whole physical through the action of the balance in the sympathetic system." This is followed with an enlightening analogy. "The sympathetic nerve system is to the soul and spirit forces as the cerebrospinal is to the physical forces of an entity" (E.C., 5717-3).

We all know that the sympathetic nerves originate in the spinal cord (or the cerebrospinal system) and go from there to the sympathetic chain or ganglia lying in front of the vertebral column, then to the organs and tissues stimulated by the sympathetic system. With this in mind, the profound influence of not only the mind, but "soul and spirit forces" as well, are brought together in a clear tripartite relationship of body, mind, and spirit.

There is a marvelous reading for a 38-year-old executive (discussed further in the chapter, *Four Cayce Patterns of Spinal Massage*) who is described as burning the candles at both ends. Nowadays we would say he is "burned out." He wasn't listening to his body's signals warning him to take it easy. Cayce said, "The sympathetic system exaggerates the condition, as a *warning* to the body, will the mental body but heed" (E.C., 5552-1). This built-in early warning system is a natural biofeedback system telling him that it can't keep his body in balance much longer if he insists on burning the candle day and night! The reading continues:

At least once each day, a *gentle* massage over the whole of the cerebrospinal and sympathetic nerve system. Not what is ordinarily termed an osteopathic massage even, though this may be given osteopathically. *Rather following the nerves of the sympathetic system,* and *manipulate* those *with* the centers of the cerebrospinal that *join* in their various centers. (E.C., 5552-1, my emphasis)

This focus on the sympathetic nervous system (and in this case the cerebrospinal also) with spinal massage puts the massage therapist in touch with the heart of that system which mediates the physical, mental, and spiritual aspects of our being. It is a crucial area of influence and central to the practice of massage. Helping the body to reach a balance between its neuromusculoskeletal system and its visceral systems facilitates states of deep relaxation and may even open a door to one's soul and spirit in the process.

The massage therapist is in a unique *relationship* with another person where there is touching, tension, change, interdependence and a need for balance and coordination. Therapist and client are welded together, moment to moment, for a brief period of time which can enhance both their lives.

Endnotes:

[1] See Rosaland E. Krauss, *Passages in Modern Sculpture*, (Cambridge, MA: MIT Press, 1981) p. 277.

[2] Ibid. p. 276.

[3] For further information see the chapter on Hydrotherapy.

[4] See Irvin Korr, D.O., "The Sympathetic Nervous System as Mediator Between the Somatic and Supportive Processes," *The Collected Papers of Irvin M. Korr*, ed. Barbara Peterson (Colorado Springs, CO: American Academy of Osteopathy, 1979).

[5] See Irvin Korr, D.O., "The Spinal Cord as Organizer of Disease Processes: The Peripheral Autonomic Nervous System," *The Collected Papers of Irvin M. Korr*, ed. Barbara Peterson (Colorado Springs, CO: American Academy of Osteopathy, 1979).

[6] William A. McGarey, M.D., *Edgar Cayce and the Palma Christi*, (Virginia Beach, VA: The Edgar Cayce Foundation, 1970) p. 65.

[7] Korr, p. 172.

[8] Ibid.

[9] Unlike a "physical reading," in which the focus is on the *body*, a "life reading" focuses on the *soul's* needs and experiences.

Chapter Three

SWEDISH, OSTEOPATHIC AND NEUROPATHIC MASSAGE

The techniques of massage have virtually remained the same for centuries. These include effleurage, friction, petrissage, tapotement, and vibration.

Effleurage is the gentle stroking movement most commonly associated with a relaxing massage. The therapist moves his or her hands (mostly the palms) over the surface of the body in a gliding, soothing motion, without friction or pressure. By varying the speed of the hands, the therapist can vary the effect, from a slow, easy, relaxing speed to a quick, light, stimulating speed.

Friction is the beginning of deep rubbing. The therapist's hands move deeper into the tissues of the body. The fingers and heels of the therapist's hands become more prominent in this motion.

Petrissage is the type of movement commonly associated with kneading. Pulling, pressing, rolling, grabbing and kneading are all forms of petrissage. This is more difficult to do well than one might first think. Often a beginner will inadvertently pinch the skin or muscle while attempting to knead or pull.

Tapotement is percussion. Tapping, cupping, slapping, striking, chopping, hacking, and pounding are all forms of tapotement.

Vibration is a rapid shaking or shimmying of tissue or limb.

These terms and descriptions remind me of Dr. Alan Stoddard's analogy between a good osteopath and a musician:

The practitioner is the artist, and the instrument is the human body. The musician can learn to play intricate melodies after he has painstakingly learned to play the scales and arpeggios. The pianist must develop his muscle power for the fortissimo passages and delicacy of touch for the pianissimo passages. So too must the osteopath learn the basic theme of normality before he can learn the variations on the original theme. He must learn the techniques of palpation, massage, and articulation before he goes on to acquire the skill of specific adjustments.

One advantage the musician has over the osteopath is that he can rely on his instrument. Unfortunately the human body is so variable an instrument that it is often impossible to play the same tune on any two spines. The player has to adapt his technique to the instrument he is playing, and he must be able to attune his own personality to that of the patient. In a busy practice he may have to adjust himself from, say, an enthusiastic golfer coming about his annoying elbow, to a deeply anxious patient worried about cancer, or to the impatient businessman who wants his neck "clicked" into place between board meetings. Such adaption requires a flexibility of mind as well of muscles on the part of the practitioner.[1]

The techniques remain virtually unchanged, but, as Dr. Stoddard points out, each body presents an entirely new environment in which the therapist must perform his art.

Generally, a massage begins on the surface of the body and gradually moves deeper. Specifically, it begins with the skin and proceeds to the subcutaneous tissue, muscle, ligaments and bones, and then to certain organs and glands. Of course, nerves, veins, arteries and capillaries are contacted at all levels of the massage.

Physiological and therapeutic effects of massage have long been associated with body tissues of the skin, the fascia, the muscular system, the nervous system. Glandular, digestive, and bony systems are also affected. The emphasis in scientific massage (massage based on anatomical structures and physiological functions) usually is on increasing or improving blood flow through veins and the absorption of lymph through lymphatic vessels, all of which thereby increase the arterial flow of blood with fresh nutrients and oxygen.

I believe it is helpful, especially to a therapist, to have a clear sense of the use and benefit of the three major methods of massage recommended by Edgar Cayce: Swedish, Osteopathic and Neuropathic.

SWEDISH MASSAGE

Swedish Massage is primarily massage of the muscular forces of the body and is usually, but not always, accompanied by some type of hot fumes bath. Generally, a Swedish Massage begins with an oil or linament rubdown and ends with an alcohol rub. This form of massage is usually very stimulating.

Swedish Massage can be traced back to the late 1700s and early 1800s and the work of Per Henrik Ling, M.D. (1776-1839). Dr. Ling developed a Swedish exercise system whose main themes remain central to present-day Swedish Massage. His system was referred to as "medical gymnastics" because it combined soft tissue manipulations and passive movements of joints based upon his studies of current anatomy and physiology. However, Dr. Ling did not like the term "massage," preferring something akin to "The Passive Motions of Medical Treatment of the Sick."[2] He believed passive motions (massage) were sufficiently stimulating and invigorating for the ill client but wanted traditional exercise for the healthy. Furthermore, he believed that massage movements should be in the direction of the heart or following the venous flow of blood.

In many respects, Dr. Ling was correct. Usually, normal physical activity produces muscle contractions which push the muscles against veins and lymph vessels aiding both venous and lymph flow toward the heart. In the absence of normal physical activity, such as times of illness or a sedentary lifestyle, decreased muscular contractions affect circulation, causing problems in tissue metabolism such as poor elimination and insufficient amounts of oxygen and nutrients to various body tissues. Massage helps overcome these situations.

Here are two Cayce readings which describe Swedish Massage.

Massage at times would be most beneficial. This given as a Swedish Massage would be more preferable than adjustments, until the body is much stronger....

Q-4. *Please explain the Swedish Massage.*

A-4. It's Swedish Massage! This is a form of massage that usually accompanies Turkish Bath treatments. It may be described as being between a neuropathic and an osteopathic and a chiropractic treatment, but it is the massaging of the muscular forces of the body – with or after fume baths, or baths where there is a rubdown afterward followed by a massage with oil and then rub alcohol.... (E.C., 289-7)

Q-4. *Just what is Swedish massage, as advised?*

A-4. That the muscular tissue and the nerve ends are kept in accord with that as is necessary for the proper functioning of limbs as related to centers of the plexus from which it receives its energy, and that the muscular tissue from each sinew – as is joined in each extremity, whether to the torso or to the extremity of the body – is rotated in such a manner as to alleviate every center through which the blood supply and nerve supply of that particular portion of the body circulates. (E.C., 5536-5)

For a 44-year-old woman, Cayce gave this suggestion:

Every week for at least a month to six weeks, have *a Swedish massage*. Don't be afraid to *get in the steam room.* You need to inhale some of the steam into your nostrils as well as into your lungs. Not too long, to be sure, the first time. But be in the steam, not your head poking out a cabinet but in the steam – only a minute to two minutes at first, then the time may be gradually increased. After this *have a thorough massage, kneading the limbs and torso, the area around the lungs, the back of neck and head.* All of these should be kneaded, not so much adjustments as a good massage. Not too much pinching but rolling, as it were, in the circular motions with the hands. For such a massage use an equal combination of Olive Oil and witchhazel. These will tend to separate, but shake together until it is thoroughly mixed each time before using, and massage thoroughly into all portions of the body. Do knead from the left side, the area of the stomach, toward the right side, pulling up the upper portion of the liver; so that we *empty the stomach well.* And we will change these conditions so that the end of the esophagus will "up" a bit and the stomach will empty much better. Also give particular reference to feet and limbs. The toes should have particular attention, especially under the toes and the bursa in front of feet, and the Achilles bursa also in the heel. Massage the oils into these areas thoroughly. (E.C., 3564-1)

OSTEOPATHIC MASSAGE

Osteopathic Massage is primarily massage of the musculoskeletal system. Generally, it focuses on balancing muscle tensions, especially as they affect the skeletal structure of the body. A particular focus is placed on relieving impingements on the cerebrospinal system by balancing muscle tension along the spinal column, thereby helping to realign the vertebrae. This type of massage is used to prepare for structural manipulations and to support the effects of the manipulations.

Osteopathy has its roots in the spiritual revelations of Dr. Andrew Taylor ("A.T.") Still. However, manipulation of the body's tissue and bones is an ancient practice, dating back at least as far as 2700 B.C. in the Far East and 1500 B.C. in the West. The Greek physician and "Father of Medicine," Hippocrates (460 to 357 B.C.), wrote many books on healing, including *Manipulation and Importance to Good Health.* But few people would disagree that Dr. A.T. Still is the "Father of Osteopathy." Dr. Still's vision is deeply spiritual and, in modern terms, holistic – viewing man physically, mentally and spiritually. Dr. Still's principles were developed after he experienced the tragic loss of his three children from meningitis.

It was when I stood gazing upon three members of my family, all dead from spinal meningitis, that I propounded to myself the serious question, In sickness, has God left man in a world of guessing? Guess what is the matter? What to give and guess the result? And when dead, guess where he goes?' I decided then, that God was not a guessing God but a God of truth. All His works spiritual and material are harmonious. His law of animal life is absolute. So wise a God had certainly placed the remedy within the material house in which the spirit of life dwells. (Quoted from his autobiography)[3]

In *Manual of Osteopathic Practice*, the author reveals the foundations and purposes of osteopathy as it developed in the mind of Dr. Still.

This tragedy in A. T. Still's life coloured all his thoughts appertaining to medicine, and he turned to religion and God to find an answer. Making the assumption that God had provided the gift of life, He must therefore provide the means of keeping the body healthy. To what should A. T. Still turn? Drugs were useless. What else was there? How did animals keep healthy? When disease affected them how did they recover? There must be some inherent healing force. How did this break down? What prevented the healing forces from working successfully in restoring health? These were the thoughts which plagued him. He had a mechanical turn of mind and had invented several mechanical devices for use on the farm where he lived. He began to think of the body as a machine. What went wrong with the machine to produce disease? Could it be that the mechanical components of the machine actually became displaced, so interfering with mechanisms of circulation and of nerve-supply?[4]

Dr. Still and Edgar Cayce agree on many major points of the nature of man, well-being, and healing. One of the best sources for such a comparison is *Osteopathy: Comparative Concepts – A.T. Still and Edgar Cayce*, by J. Gail Cayce (the granddaughter of Edgar Cayce). Here are some of their key points of agreement.

On the idea of self-healing:
Still: All remedies necessary to good health exist in the human body. They can be administered by adjusting the body in such a way that the remedies may naturally associate themselves together. (A.T. Still[5])
Cayce: But nature's store house (thine own body) may be induced to create every influence necessary for bringing

55

greater and better and nearer normal conditions, if the hindrances are removed. (E.C., 1309-1)

On the idea of natural laws and the forces of Nature:
Still: The osteopath who succeeds best does so because he looks to Nature for knowledge and obeys her teaching, then he gets good results. He is often amazed to see how faithfully Nature sticks to system. A few years spent in the school of Nature teaches the osteopath that principles govern the universe, and he must obey all orders, or fail to cure his patients. We say disease when we should say effect; for disease is the effect of change in the parts of the physical body. (A.T. Still[6])

Cayce: Thus the interests of the entity in activities in which there may be the use of mechanical as well as other means for the correcting of deformities or those tenets and truths of that organization in which the entity applies self – create the proper vibrations, coordinating the organs of the body-mind, and letting nature do the healing. By nature here we mean the natural sources, or God's sources. These are correct. Hold close to them. (E.C., 3394-2)

On the influence of electrical impulses:
Still: On whom or what does this engine [man] depend for its motive force? ... All must have and cannot act without the highest known order of force (electricity), which submits to the voluntary and involuntary commands of life and mind, by which worlds are driven and beings move. (A.T. Still[7])

Cayce: As we may see in a functioning physical organism, electricity in its incipiency or lowest form is the nearest vibration in a physical sense to Life itself; for it is the nucleus about each atom of active force or principle set by the atomic activity of blood pulsation itself, that begins from the union of the plasm that creates life itself in a physical organism. (E.C., 3990-1)

On the importance of good blood supply:
Still: In the year 1874 I proclaimed that a disturbed artery marked the beginning to an hour and a minute when disease

began to sow its seeds of destruction in the human body. That in no case could it be done without a broken or suspended current of arterial blood, which by nature was intended to supply and nourish all nerves, ligaments, muscles, skin, bones, and the artery itself. (A.T. Still[8])

Cayce: ... there is no condition existent in a body that the reflection of same may not be traced in the blood supply, for not only does the blood stream carry the rebuilding forces to the body; it also takes the used forces and eliminates same through their proper channels in the various portions of the system. Hence we find red blood, white blood and lymph all carried in the veins. These are only separated by the very small portions that act as builders, strainers, destroyers or resuscitating portions of the system .... Hence there is ever seen in the blood stream the reflection or evidences of that condition being carried on in the physical body. (E.C., 283-2)

And, finally, on the nature and importance of osteopathy:

Still: What is the object of moving bones, muscles, and ligaments, which are suspending the powers of the nerves and so on? A very common answer is, to loosen up all spaces through which nerves, veins, and arteries convey elements of life and motion. If that be your answer, then you have fallen far short of an answer that is based on a knowledge of the basic principles of life in beings, its methods of preparing to repair some part, organ, limb, or the whole system. If an over-accumulation should appear and obstruct the process of life to annoy the normal harmony to such measure as to produce unrest or disease, would you or I be satisfied to know we had simply given the sufferer a good shaking up, had pulled the arms and legs ... and kneaded the chest, limbs, and abdomen, as we have done and do so many times a day or week? No, we would renovate first by lymph, giving it time to do its work of atomizing all crudities first.... If life be aided in the process of renovating all hindrances to health ... call forth lymph, fibrin, albumin, uric acid, muriatic, or any fluid from the great chemical laboratory of man's machinery.... (A.T. Still[9])

Cayce: As a *system* of treating human ills, osteopathy –

WE would give – is more beneficial than most measures that may be given. Why? In any preventative or curative measure, that condition to be produced is to assist the system to gain its normal equilibrium. It is known that each organ receives impulses from other portions of the system by the suggestive forces (sympathetic nervous system) and by circulatory forces (the cerebrospinal system and the blood supply itself). These course through the system in very close parallel activity in EVERY single portion of the body.

Hence stimulating ganglia from which impulses arise – either sympathetically or functionally – must then be helpful in the body gaining an equilibrium." (E.C., 902-1)

Then, the SCIENCE of osteopathy is not merely the punching in a certain segment or the cracking of the bones, but it is the keeping of a BALANCE – by the touch – between the sympathetic and the cerebrospinal system! THAT is real osteopathy!

With the adjustments made in this way and manner, we will find not only helpful influences but healing and an aid to any condition that may exist in the body (unless there is a broken bone or the like)! (E.C., 1158-24))

From this we can assume that a good osteopathic massage strives to recreate the lost harmony between sympathetic and cerebrospinal, to stimulate natural forces within the body to remove the blockages to equilibrium and flow, and to "call forth" the natural fluids and forces of the body to do their good work again. In practice, this means we must have a good understanding of the location of the important parts of the body (i.e., sympathetic, cerebrospinal, lymph, viscera, arteries, veins, etc.). We must have an understanding of how best to manipulate these areas in order to create the actions we seek. As Dr. Still says,

Osteopathy is that science which consists of such exact, exhaustive, and verifiable knowledge of the structure and functions of the human mechanism, anatomical, physiological and psychological, including the chemistry and physics of its known elements, and has made discoverable certain organic laws and remedial resources, within the body itself, by which nature under the scientific treatment peculiar to osteopathic practice, apart from all ordinary methods of extraneous, artificial, or medicinal stimulation, and in harmonious accord with its own mechanical principles, molecular activities, and metabolic processes, may recover from displacements, disorganizations, derangements, and consequent disease, and regain its normal equilibrium of form and function in health and strength.[10]

Of course, for much of this, the deeper study would be left to the professional practitioner. However, the Cayce readings encourage every person to gain a basic understanding of the temple in which they abide (their body) if they would receive the full benefit of a whole, healthy life.

NEUROPATHIC MASSAGE

Neuropathy is a form of drugless therapy treatment developed at the turn of the century. Its foremost school, the American College of Neuropathy, was established in 1907. According to one of its earlier practitioners, "Neuropathy is that science of the healing art by which all diseased conditions of each and every part of the body are restored to health by regulating the blood supply to the involved areas through the nerve mechanism."[11] Neuropathy emphasizes lymphatic drainage and control of circulation by stimulating reflex effects to vaso-constrictors and vaso-dilators. With lymph and blood circulation crucial to a healthy body, "the first step in a Neuropathic treatment is relieving lymphatic stasis."[12] Then treatment is given to "nerve centers controlling circulation for the purpose of restoring the normal activity to the vaso-motor nerves"[13] using sedation or stimulation techniques as required.

Neuropathic massage is primarily massage of the nervous system throughout the body. Using various massage strokes, its goal is to improve circulation and the flow of nerve impluses.

In *Massage and Therapeutic Exercise* (1932) by Mary McMillan, the author says: "The motor and sensory nerves of the cerebrospinal system and of the autonomic or sympathetic system may be stimulated or soothed according to the character of the manipulation used." (p.18) This concept is also given great emphasis in the Edgar Cayce readings.

In *Massage: Its Principles and Technic*, by Max Bohm, M. D., an entire chapter is devoted to "Massage of the Nerves and Skin."[14] For example, in cases of neuritis and neuralgia where there is usually a great deal of pain, Bohm recommends "nerve massage" when inflammation subsides: "This consists, first, in regular massage (effleurage, petrissage, and tapotement) of the limb supplied by the nerve attached. Afterward one may approach the nerve as far as it is accessible, effleuraging it along its course, seeking to reach the places especially painful (point douloureuse), using friction and vibration. This treatment may be finished by a gentle tapotement of the nerve." (p. 78 ff.)

Dr. John H. Kellogg, in *The Art of Massage*, writes about the technique of nerve compression. This is the application of pressure along a nerve fiber, especially at points called "motor points" which are near the surface of the body. Or pressure may be applied to the spinal nerves with two fingers, one on each side of the spine. Physiological effects depend upon the amount of pressure and length of time of nerve compression. Light and brief pressure with repetition stimulates the nerve points and its centers. A firmer, deeper pressure continued for a longer time tends to produce numbness and a sedative effect. Kellogg even describes stimulation of the lumbar ganglia and subumbilical ganglion deep within the abdominal cavity and anterior to the spine.

Dr. Kellogg also refers to effects on nerve centers when discussing friction. He claims that the primary effect of friction is to venous blood flow and the lymph system, but he also includes nerve centers. For example:

To promote absorption, rub toward the heart (centripetal friction). For sedative and derivative effects upon the viscera and nerve centers, rub downward (centrifugal friction). Rubbing upward, or in the direction of the venous blood current, increases the activity of the circulation. Rubbing downward decreases vascular activity.[15]

Dr. Kellogg stresses the importance of rate of movement and direction of movement with the effects mentioned above. He also describes different forms of friction (i.e., a deep rubbing motion), such as Circular Friction, Spiral Friction, and Rotary Friction.

Circular Friction is applicable to the extremities. A limb is grasped by both hands, and, with an alternating wringing or twisting movement, the therapist begins at the extremity (hand or foot) and moves up the limb toward the body.

Spiral Friction is executed with one hand using a spiral motion, moving from the lower (or distal) to the upper (or proximal) end of the body part.

Rotary Friction is moving one or both hands over a broad surface in an elliptical, circular or semicircular direction; especially applicable to such fleshy areas as the hip and back.

Each of these is significant in relation to the Edgar Cayce readings which frequently describe different forms of neuromassage. I am using the term *neuromassage* to describe all those readings in which directions for massage are usually given in one of three ways:

1) massage with "a rotary motion on either side of the cerebrospinal system or spinal column" (E.C., 1618-1);

2) "massage in a circular motion along both sides of the spinal system" (E.C., 2491-1);

3) "massage [of] the lower portion of the spine gently *in a neuropathic manner*, circular on either side of the spine" (E.C., 1168-1).

When a Cayce reading suggests neuropathic massage, the emphasis is always on circular massage following the nervous system, but not all readings suggesting massage with a rotary or circular motion are referred to as "neuropathic massage." Therefore, I am using the word *neuromassage* to describe the application of massage techniques to the nervous system for deep relaxation, coordination, and balance of different body systems — not just the nervous system and the "blood supply." The word *neuropathic* contains the root *pathos* meaning "suffering or disease of the nerves." Although my examples of neuromassage are from the readings of people with illnesses, I want to eventually suggest that this form of massage be used for relaxation and general well-being.

The Cayce readings suggest that the purposes and effects of neuromassage go beyond the practice of neuropathy. They include the following:

1) To stimulate nerve impulses from nerve centers and ganglia to functioning portions of the body (E.C., 1553-5)

2) To aid mental or soul force and physical coordination (E.C., 1553-5; E.C., 5717-3)

3) To assist the absorption or assimilation of forces such as gold (E.C., 1533-5), Atomidine[16] (E.C., 548-1), and oils (E.C., 372-8)

4) To stimulate the nerve branches between the cerebrospinal and sympathetic ganglia alongside the spinal column (E.C., 2456-4)

5) To make for coordinate activity between the cerebrospinal and sympathetic nervous system (E.C., 920-8)

6) To make for coordinate activity of centers or plexuses along the spine (E.C., 920-8)

7) To stimulate the circulatory system (E.C., 920-9; E.C., 88-1; E.C., 1300-2)

8) To aid relaxation (E.C., 2491-1; E.C., 88-1)

9) To increase capillary & arterial circulation (E.C., 357-1).

What these all have in common is the effect of coordination – the coordinating of one part of the body with another and one type of treatment with another to make the application of a medicinal substance or electrical device more effective. Although 2), 3), and 4) above are perhaps unique to Cayce, they all need to be explored further.

Let's look at three readings from the Edgar Cayce files.

Mr. C: Yes. As we find the body in the present is showing some improvements. The disturbance has been rather the inability of the body to produce sufficient blood cells, through the destruction of cellular forces in structural body that aid in the creation of blood cells. Thus the inability – through the condition of the blood stream, the gland forces and structural body – to produce or to increase the numbers of cellular forces for the body – or the blood cells.

Hence deterioration or emaciation has been experienced in portions of the body.

We find that these applications, if kept in the right proportion, would offer better opportunities for the body:

Once each week, say on Thursdays, we would use the Infra Red Light. This may be given for thirty minutes in the beginning and gradually increased to sixty minutes – that is after it has been used for serveral weeks.

Daily, we would also use the Ultra-Violet Light. Do not use this, however, without the projection of the green glass between the Light and the body. Begin with a minute and gradually increase – after some time – to a minute and a half to three or three and a half minutes; that is after a week to two weeks, these may be lessened in frequency and given for longer periods. Do not give the Ultra-Violet the same day that the Infra-Red is given. It may be given every day except Thursdays and Sundays.

Each day following the Light treatment have a gentle massage; this not to make corrections in structural portions of the body, but more as would be given by a masseuse – but carefully along the whole spinal area and especially those areas where the rib centers connect with the spinal column. Give this especially *along the areas where the sympathetic nerve system connects directly with the ganglia of the cerebrospinal centers* – especially, then, in the 3rd and 4th cervical, 1st, 2nd, 3rd dorsal, 5th and 6th dorsal, 9th dorsal and through the sacral and lumbar areas. *These massages would be of a relaxing nature, causing greater flow of impulse of the nervous forces to the general forces of the body itself.* (E.C., 3191-1)

For a 21-year-old female:

Through manipulation that may be given by the electrically driven vibrator, make those relaxations in the 3rd, 4th and 5th dorsal area, sufficient that the stomach itself may be pushed – as it were – or drawn, by the contraction of the muscular forces created by the enlivening of these particular centers, to its normal position....

We would also use the violet ray over the whole cerebro-spinal system, following a gentle massage that may be given over the body; and *especially* should this be given over the lower portion of the cerebro-spinal system, particularly in the lower dorsal, lumbar and sacral area....

Give the violet ray each evening, *following* the massage. The massage need not necessarily be made as corrective measure osteopathically, but may be more in the nature of the neuropathic. Begin at the base of brain and go *towards* the central portion of body. Begin at the lower limbs and go (along the muscular forces on the inside, or following out the sciatic nerve centers along the inside of the limbs) to the trunk portion of body. Then along the cerebro-spinal system to the middle portion. Then we would give the violet ray for three to ten minutes each evening. This will so stimulate the circulation to the exterior portions, and vitalize the whole activities through an increased activity of the assimilated forces of the system, as to bring the proper balance in the body.... (E.C., 263-1)

Here's another important reading:

Mr. C: Yes, we have the body here, [1413]; this we have had before.

As we find, while there are still many conditions that must be changed for the better reactions and for the corrections in the system, the body is a little bit on the improve – though there are periods of the violent reaction and the attempts of the system to eliminate poisons, as the sympathetic system becomes imbued with same through the incoordination between the sympathetic and the cerebrospinal systems.

Hence these changes as we find we would make;

First in the manipulations and massage; Every third treatment, at least, we would make specific adjustments, now, in those centers where the cerebrospinal AND the sympathetic nerve systems react the more specifically together; notably in the 4th lumbar, the 9th dorsal, the 1st and 2nd dorsal, and through the 3rd and 4th and 2nd cervical MAKE DEFINITE adjustments by MOVING – at least – the segments in these areas. The other treatments or daily treatments besides this we find are well....

Let these applications be made by that one giving the massages. And after each treatment with the Appliance, give a THOROUGH MASSAGE NEUROPATHICALLY over the WHOLE BODY, where it is possible or practical to treat. This as we find will aid in the system's absorbing the activities to create not only a normal balance with the correction in the centers indicated, but to make for a balance in the glandular activities of the body as to prevent the salts of the system becoming overbalanced and so susceptible to the activities from without....

Hence the manipulations or the neuropathic manipulations following each treatment thoroughly over the system. Stimulate all centers, all ganglia, all the activities through the system, both to the lymph and the emunctory circulation where they come close to the surface in the superficial circulation – where the stimulation is so needed; that the vibrations created (through the use of the Appliance) may be DISTRIBUTED THROUGHOUT THE BODY ITSELF.... (E.C., 1413-3)

These readings, among many others, illustrate the versatility of neuromassage in effecting treatment for diverse individuals and ailments alike. In the next chapter, we will further discuss spinal massage patterns.

Endnotes:

[1] Alan Stoddard, M.B., B.S., D.O., M.D., *Manual of Osteopathic Practice* (New York: Harper & Row, 1969).

[2] Armand Maanum with Herb Montgomery, *The Complete Book of Swedish Massage* (Minneopolis, MN: Winston Press, 1985) p. 2 ff.

[3] Andrew T. Still, D.O., *Autobiography of A.T. Still* (Kirksville, MO: Published by the Author, 1897).

[4] Stoddard, p. xv.

[5] J. Gail Cayce, *Osteopathy: Comparative Concepts –A.T. Still and Edgar Cayce* (Virginia Beach, VA: Edgar Cayce Foundation, 1973) p. 5.

[6] Ibid., p. 7.

[7] Ibid., p. 9.

8 Ibid., p. 16.

9 Ibid., p. 38.

10 Ibid., p. 39.

11 Thomas T. Lake, N.D., D.C. , *Treatment by Neuropathy & the Encyclopedia of Physical and Manipulative Therapeutic* (Publisher unknown, 1946) p. 193. [Editors note: This is one of those obscure, out-of-print, treasurers that Joseph Duggan loved. We found a copy in the Learning Resources Center of the National College Chiropractic Center in Lombard, IL. Copies are also in the National Library of Medicine. See appendix for addresses.]

12 Ibid, p.17

13 Ibid, p.149

14 Max Bohm, M.D. (Ed.), *Massage: Its Principles and Technic* (Philadephia, PA: W.B. Sauners & Co, 1913).

15 John H. Kellogg, *The Art of Massage* (Battle Creek, MI: Modern Medicine Publishing Co., 1895) p. 193.

16 Atomidine is an atomic form of iodine often recommended in the readings for internal use to help balance glandular activity, always in extremely *small* doses. However, its use can be dangerous. Therefore, I suggest you do not use or recommend this until you have a full understanding of the manner and proportions Cayce gave. Of course, any time internal use is recommended I believe you should not proceed to ingest the item until you are sure you understand its purpose, effect and the manner and proportion by which it is to be used. Even then, your particular body or the combination with other medicines you may be using might cause a reaction quite different from that described. So be careful and fully informed.

Chapter Four

FOUR CAYCE PATTERNS OF SPINAL MASSAGE

Spinal massage is given directly on the spine along the cerebrospinal system over the sympathetic chain of ganglia (about one inch away from the center of the spine on each side; see illustration 7), over major nerve plexuses along the spine, and along nerve pathways emanating from major plexuses relating to arm and leg movement.

The Edgar Cayce readings not only recommend massage as one of the most frequent treatments to promote good health, but give specific directions for spinal massage in hundreds of readings. When categorized, these directions fit into one of four major massage patterns. The first describes a massage beginning at the base of the brain and working downward along the sides of the spine and out towards the extremities. The second moves from the extremities toward the ninth dorsal or solar plexus. The third begins in the middle of the spine (solar plexus) and works toward the head and out the arms and then again from the middle of the spine down the spine and out the legs. The fourth type describes a circular massage beginning at the base of the spine and proceeding upward along the sides of the spine.

In Cayce's holistic approach to health, we are given information in the readings outside the standard clinical domain. For example, each reading described here includes directions for massage, but other factors pertaining to health – stress, for example – are likewise mentioned. For this reason, I include background data available on these individuals as well as pertinent information relating to their physical condition. Cayce offers us much to learn, both in the practice of massage therapy and in our own personal growth.

Now lets's study each pattern individually.

DOWN THE SPINE

Far and away, the most frequently given pattern for massage is *down the spine*. Its purpose, unless otherwise stated in a reading, is to stimulate circulation and affect the autonomic nervous system for a better coordination. It's safe to assume that most individuals would benefit from this type of massage properly given.

Let's look at a reading that includes an excellent description of a gentle neuropathic massage so often recommended in the readings.

Then, to act together with the reactions to the assimilating system, we would have the *neuropathic massage* – which would be helpful. But when such massages are given, we would use a combination of oils prepared in this manner:

To 6 ounces of Russian White Oil as the base, add – in the order named:

> Kerosene Oil, 1 ounce
> Camphor...Gum Camphor, but dissolved, 1/2 ounce
> Oil of Cedar Wood, 1/2 ounce
> Oil of Pine Needles, 1/2 ounce
> Oil of Sassafras, 1/4 ounce

To be sure, when standing these will tend to separate. When they are to be used, (once or twice a day in the beginning), shake together and pour a quantity into an open container – but keep away from the fire, of course; using each time just what will be massaged into the body. Massage or work from the body, not toward the body. *Begin at the base of the brain and work in a circular motion down either side of the cerebrospinal system.* When coming to the *brachial center,* let the massage extend also around the upper portion of the rib – or to those centers that come to the central portion, or to the sternum, or to the frontal portion in the lung area itself. When coming to the *9th dorsal,* then extend the massage – of course – around that line about the body, or the lower portion of the diaphragm area. Also at the *4th lumbar center,* let it extend to those edges above the hip bone to the frontal part. *Then carry on through to the feet,* just what the body will absorb of the solution. (E.C., 1127-1)

This is clearly not a "general massage" using effleurage and petrissage techniques which emphasize blood and lymph flow. This person's muscles and ligaments were already atrophied; (we will discuss his physical condition below). The circular motion of the massage downward is a type of friction, but clearly not with the effects suggested by Dr. Kellogg of sedation and decreased vascular flow. It is more like Mary McMillan's suggestion of stimulation to the cerebrospinal and sympathetic nervous systems and the purposes of neuropathy – to regulate blood supply through stimulation of nerve impulses. (See *Neuropathic Massage* in chapter on Swedish, Osteopathic and Neuropathic Massage.)

It is significant to learn that this reading was given for a 43-year-old man diagnosed by his physician as having a "weeping paresis"; the readings suggest *muscular dystrophy*.[1] This affords us the opportunity to better understand the effects of massage on the internal body systems and the role of massage in the treatment of muscular dystrophy.

Dr. Bill McGarey has extensively researched the Edgar Cayce readings on this disease. According to his findings,[2] the etiology given in the readings indicates that muscular dystrophy is primarily a glandular malfunction. This, in turn, affects the normal growth of nerve tissue which then affects muscle tissue. In late stages of the disease there is "more atrophy of the nerves which control the muscular forces of the body" (E.C., 5078-1).

The first suggestion in 1127's readings is to take Calcidin to help with assimilation of calcium and iodine. Assuming the classification in the Index under "Muscular Dystrophy" is accurate, this would help stimulate the glandular system which would then aid nerve impulses to the involved muscle tissue. The massage would stimulate the autonomic nervous system and those centers or nerve plexuses which send nerve impulses to the extremities and to the abdominal area to aid assimilation. In Neuropathic massage, then, the direction of the strokes – massaging "from the body, not toward the body," as Cayce directed – stimulates the nervous system. This includes both the spinal nerves of the central nervous system (cerebrospinal nervous system), the sympathetic ganglia alongside the spinal column, the brachial and lumbar plexuses, nerves along the back of the legs, and the lower part of the diaphragm area.

Clearly, the purpose of neuromassage/neuropathic massage here is to:

1) assist assimilations

2) stimulate nerve impulses passing through plexuses

3) stimulate nerve impulses along nerve fibers to extremities

4) stimulate peristalsis (the lower diaphragm area).

Similar suggestions for massage are given in the next reading. The only difference is that the massage is confined to the spine. Yet, as you will see, the goals for treatment are quite different.

A father had sought Cayce's help for his son; the boy was dying from leukemia. Cayce's reading traced the source of his condition to "primarily a glandular activity" causing an infection in the spleen, which was enlarged, and in the lymph. Also, certain centers along the cerebrospinal nervous system had become static — those which help produce red blood cells from rib bone marrow. A deficiency in iodine was also noted. Treatment included: 1) the taking of Atomidine internally, 2) use of infra-red heat over the cerebrospinal area followed immediately with a peanut oil massage "along the spine," 3) dietary recommendations for liver pudding and orange juice, and 4) the injunction to keep an attitude helpful to healing.

Regarding the massage, here is what was said:

Q-7. Was the massage given heavy enough? How long should it be given?

A-7. *The massage* is very well, but we would do this the more often, see? As long as there is an opportunity of it producing the effect to all areas of the better activity to the organs of the body. The *"Why"* of the massage should be considered: Inactivity causes many of those portions along the spine from which impulses are received to the various organs to be lax, or taut, or to allow some to receive greater impulse than others. The massage aids [stimulates] the ganglia to receive impulses from nerve forces as it aids circulation [and assimilation] through the various portions of the organism. (E.C., 2456-4)

The boy was hospitalized and had been receiving blood transfusions to increase his blood platelet count. A subsequent reading indicated that the massage would "assist the body in assimilating the transfusions, as well as to stimulate the organs of distribution and assimilation to aid body-building" (E.C., 2456-5).

A glandular problem was the cause of disease in both the boy and the man with muscular dystrophy (1127), discussed earlier. Both needed stimulation of the nerves via massage – the boy, for circulation; the man; for his muscles. In the former, the blood content was out of balance. In the latter, there was nerve damage. A portion of the system had become lax or static in both.

In October, 1940, Cayce received a letter from a woman requesting a reading for her brother who she described as being "completely out of his mind." Confined to a sanitarium at the time of the reading, he was very weak – eating almost nothing – and had a paralyzed bladder. He had been tied to his bed because of violent outbursts that kept him from getting any rest.

When the sister received the reading and went to the sanitarium for the first time, she discovered that her brother had been put in a special room because of his violent and erratic behavior – shouting, walking the floor all night, and saying he was crazy. He was now being force-fed through the nostrils, and had been catheterized.

His doctors gave conflicting diagnoses. One thought his mental behavior was due to a physical cause, the other believed he may have had a "nervous collapse."

Cayce's reading (2387-1) attributes the problem to a "general nervous collapse" – a breakdown between the cerebrospinal system's coordination with the sympathatic nervous system "due to the absence of those vital energies" which flow down along the cerebrospinal system. The "vital

71

energies" referred to here are those life energies of mind and spirit that cannot be explained by physics and chemistry alone.

The resultant physical and mental collapse caused an incoordination of activity in the area of the 9th dorsal. Catheterization had caused uremic poisoning; in addition, dehydration was ensuing. If something wasn't done soon, Cayce's prognosis was insanity due to imminent hemorrhaging in the brain!

This reading is a clear example of Dr. Irvin Korr's thesis that the sympathetic nervous system functions as a mediator or a tuner among the musculoskeletal system, the viscera, and impulses from the higher centers – the brain, mind and soul forces.[3] Dr. Korr points out that human activity is made up of continually changing patterns of muscle and bone. Our behavior, what we do – whether moral, philosophical, practical or religious – involves the many contractile possibilities of our muscles. It is this activity which distinguishes one behavior from another, each unique individual from another and, in essence, defines us as human beings. Dr. Korr says, "I came to view the neuromusculoskeletal system as a primary machinery of life."[4] Therefore, any demands on the *primary machinery of life* that can't be met by coordinating them with the support system (the viscera) results in illness.

Obviously, Mr. 2387's bizarre behavior and accompanying neuromusculoskeletal activity reflected not only a mental and emotional breakdown, but impaired communication within his body. His support system couldn't maintain the kind of behavior demanded over long periods of time; it was too stressful. Nor could he communicate or relate to others in a successful or healthy way. The point in all this is that any one part of the system – musculoskeletal, viscera, or higher centers – may be the original cause of the problem or illness. But over a period of time, one or more of the other parts can become involved and a vicious cycle is set up. 2387's emotional breakdown led to an incoordination between his cerebrospinal and sympathetic nervous system; specifically, in the area of the 9th dorsal. Kidney paralysis and uremic poisoning followed. From emotional pain to physical pain – around and around.

The treatment plan for 2387 was simple, given its remarkable results and the severity of his condition: apply turpentine stupes[5] to restore normal urination, drink beef juice for strength, and give a "spinal rub" – a massage from the base of the brain to the end of the spine – when the body begins to respond.

A second reading given within ten days indicated that the catheter had already been removed; the brother was improving. Again, a spinal rub was recommended.

Each evening, for twenty to thirty minutes, give a spinal rub. This would be given – by the nurse – when the body is prepared for sleeping, or for bed. Rub with pure Peanut Oil, in a circular motion, down either side of the spine (illustration 13). This will not only aid in the absorption of this to create a better superficial circulation, but will aid in making better coordinations between the reflexes of the sympathetic system AND the cerebrospinal system. (E.C., 2387-2)

Three important concepts can be gleaned from this reading regarding the value of spinal massage not only for 2387, but for others, as well. First, given when preparing to sleep, massage facilitates relaxation and the release of tension by relieving pressures along the spine. Second, spinal massage helps stimulate the absorption of peanut oil, an oil which helps stimulate the superficial circulation. And third, the spinal rub helps coordinate or balance the cerebrospinal and sympathetic nervous systems.

In about five weeks, a third reading was given; 2387 had taken a turn for the worse. Cayce recommended Atomidine for the glandular system, the use of stupes again for the bladder, and osteopathy for the 9th dorsal center.

Letters from 2387's sister to Edgar Cayce over the next two years described his gradual improvement. He had been moved from the sanitarium to Massachusetts General Hospital in Boston with a diagnosis of "involutional depression." From Boston he went with his wife to Florida for a vacation. Although much better, he still carried a lot of tension. His sister wrote: "He is still very nervous and quite tense, and he is likely to be so until he becomes absorbed in an interest." Nevertheless, his journey from near insanity and possible death from hemorrhaging to a near normal condition speaks for itself.

The next reading, for a 24-year-old male, is important because it gives the reasons for spinal massage and coordination between the sympathetic and cerebrospinal systems. The illustrations in the center of this book should be helpful in following Cayce's anatomical references.

Mr. C: Yes, we have the body here, [3075].

As we find, the conditions that disturb this body are as much of a psychological nature as of a pathological nature.

Pathologically, these would have to do with conditions which existed during the period of gestation.

Psychologically, these have to do with the karma of this body, and those responsible for the physical body.

Hence we have here conditions that at times approach near to that of possession of the mind by external influences, or that very close to the spiritual possession by disincarnate forces.

To be sure, these interpretations would not be accepted by some as an explanation. And yet there will come those days when many will understand and interpret properly.

As we find from here, these are the pathological reactions:

Owing to those conditions which existed in the manner in which coordination is established in the physical reactions between impressions received through sensory system and the reaction upon the reflexes of brain, we find these at times become very much dis-associated. And those impressions received sympathetically, or through vision, through hearing, through sensing by impressions, become the motivative force in the reaction.

At such times possession near takes place.

With the capsule of the inner brain itself, these cause the distortions, the associations with not the normal reflexes but with the impressions received in the suggestive forces.

Hence, as we find, with patience these may be materially aided. Then, these would be the manners:

Select some good hypnotist, such as Garrett or Kuhn, or both, and have the body put under those influences.

When aroused from this subjection of the subconscious to control, by the performing of such impressions, use the low electrical forces to change vibrations through the body. The hand machine violet ray should be sufficient. Apply the bulb applicator of this principally to the 9th dorsal, 3rd cervical, and the base of the brain. Not too long a period, just sufficient to dis-associate the flexes as would nominally come as there is the regaining of the NORMAL reactions of the body.

Follow this with a *gentle massage*, that stimulates or relaxes by the *stimulation of each of the ganglia along the cerebrospinal system*; more specifically in the areas where the cerebrospinal and sympathetic coordinate – in the larger forms of the ganglia. These we find in the 1st, 2nd and 3rd cervical, 1st, 2nd and 3rd dorsal, 9th dorsal, and in the lumbar axis and coccyx center.

Q-7. Should the massage be osteopathic, or could it be given by someone other than an osteopath?

A-7. Anyone that understands the anatomical structure of the body, in knowing how to coordinate the sympathetic and cerebrospinal systems in the areas indicated. These are not merely to be punched or pressed, but the ganglia – while very small – are as networks in these various areas. Hence a gentle, circular massage is needed; using only at times structural portions as leverages, but not ever – of course – bruising structure. (E.C., 3075-1)

The references to spinal massage in this case are significant for three reasons: 1) circular massage along the cerebrospinal system actually stimulates each of the sympathetic ganglia along the spinal column; 2) this stimulation is particularly effective in specific areas of the spine; that is, the 1st, 2nd, and 3rd cervical, 1st, 2nd, 3rd, and 9th dorsal, the lumbar axis, and the coccyx – areas of maximum coordination between the sympathetic and cerebrospinal systems because of large ganglia; and 3) the spinal massage can be either stimulating or relaxing, depending upon the needs of the body.

In 1929, a well-known business executive wrote to Edgar Cayce requesting a reading for his friend, a 38-year-old executive with nervous exhaustion. "This will introduce to you a very dear friend of mine of long standing," the letter stated. " He has been burning the candles at both ends just as I have been doing in the past several years."

So many of us are guilty of this way of life these days. Here we have the opportunity to study stress and suggestions given to alleviate it as presented in the Edgar Cayce readings.[6]

The businessman entered the Cayce hospital on November 7, 1929. His reading (5552-1) indicates that he sometimes had low blood pressure, then high blood pressure. The nervous system was "so overtaxed that at times the whole of the functional system refuses to work!" Stomach troubles caused regurgitation and lung problems created feelings of depression. There was at times a dryness in his throat. The reading's declaration that these conditions "shouldn't amount to anything" further illustrates how overwhelming stress can be even though it is easily treatable. Apparently, the man was so confused by these sensations he could no longer discern whether they were real or imagined.

Not that the conditions are imaginary, no! Rather that the sympathetic [nervous] system *exaggerates* the condition, as a *warning* to the body, will the mental body but heed, taking *advantage* of the conditions being active, and will the body use discretion and use the proper precautions *before* there *are* such conditions as *become* organic – through constant strain. The body may build into the system a full, whole, resuscitation to the physical functioning of the body. (E.C., 5552-1)

The treatments for this executive might easily have come from a book on holistic health: a gentle massage, osteopathic adjustments, fresh air and exercise by walking or biking or golfing, eating when hungry, and keeping "the mind *active*, but *blank*." Sweat baths and salt rubs were also suggested. Undoubtedly, biofeedback would have been part of the prescription had it been available in those days.[7]

Although the direction of the massage isn't specified in

the executive's reading, I feel we can safely assume it's "downward" for two reasons. First, most readings recommending "gentle massage" or massage along the spine say to massage downward. Secondly, when the emphasis is on the sympathetic nervous system, as is the case here, the direction is usually downward. The following reading is exemplary:

Massage in a gentle circular motion with this [Cocoa Butter] all the way to the end of the spine. Never up and down, but a circular motion coming down always, on either side of the spine (illustration 13); so that the reaction of this is to the sympathetic system (illustration 7), rather than the cerebrospinal.(E.C.9560-10)

So massage downward, along the spine, has a balancing effect on the warring components of the autonomic nervous system – that system which can control body activities automatically, such as heart rate, digestion, and breathing. These need to be in a state of equilibrium, not in disharmony and constant agitation because of overwork, worry and lack of exercise.

Our executive stayed in the Cayce Hospital for one week, receiving the treatments suggested in his reading and resting. On the day he was discharged from the hospital, his chart read: "Out playing golf." He was obviously on his way to a more balanced approach to life.

TOWARD THE SOLAR PLEXUS

Spinal massage towards the solar plexus – from the head down to the 9th dorsal and from the end of the spine up to the 9th dorsal – affects the cerebrospinal system through relaxation and the releasing of congestion in nerve centers and plexuses. (It does not stimulate superficial and deep circulation.) A primary function is to promote drainage, which will be discussed later.

Any massage technique that works toward the middle of the back or away from it is going to lack a certain continuity, smoothness and flow. Strokes which move up or down the entire length of the spine covering the entire back with one

77

movement, or which follow muscle groupings or venous flow, feel smoother, more comfortable, coordinated and relaxing. Why change these timeless techniques, and what would be the effect?

As far as I know, there are no techniques anywhere in the history of massage describing a spinal massage beginning at the base of the brain and the end of the spine and working *toward* the center of the back, specifically the 9th dorsal, the solar plexus center (illustration 10). However, I have found five Edgar Cayce readings which recommend massage along the spine toward the 9th dorsal. Here is an example:

> After each of the treatments given with the low electrical vibration[8] (that is, each evening), massage the body *gently* with equal portions of Olive Oil and Tincture of Myrrh, from the base of the brain to the 9th dorsal, from the end of the spine of the coccyx area to the center or to the 9th dorsal area – just what the body absorbs. But let the massage be in a rotary motion sufficient that each of the ganglia along the cerebrospinal system receives an impulse from the vibrations of the properties used. (E.C., 1134-1)

In comparing the five cases, there are some interesting characteristics. Cayce discusses each person as having some kind of incoordination between the cerebrospinal and sympathetic nervous systems, as so often was the case. Whether this is a cause or an effect, however, differs in each case. Other similar symptoms included nervousness, lack of strength and difficulty of locomotion. The remaining symptoms were individual: glandular disturbances, heart problems, circulation difficulties, deterioration of nerve plexuses, psoriasis, thinned walls of blood vessels, poor eliminations and assimilations, and others.

Two of the recommendations for treatments remained constant in each case: the use of the Wet Cell Appliance[9] and massage along the spine *towards* the solar plexus or the 9th dorsal vertebra. Looking at illustrations 10, 14, 6 and 7, in that order, can help us understand the significance of this massage pattern.

First, there are four parts to the massage:

1) C_1 to T_9 right side
2) C_1 to T_9 left side
3) Coccyx to T_9 right side
4) Coccyx to T_9 left side.

Massage strokes should be of a circular motion from the brachial and lumbar plexuses toward the solar plexus. Massaging the sympathetic ganglia stimulates nerve impulses to the plexuses.

A second consideration may be deduced from osteopathy. Osteopathic treatments are often given for the purpose of setting up "drainages," especially what is called osteopathic massage. Instead of movements of vertebrae and adjustments, osteopathic massage concentrates on massage and manipulation of ganglia and plexuses along the spine, and manipulation of muscles, tendons, bursae and nerves in the brachial, lumbar and sacral plexuses.

Q-7. What is the meaning of drainage?

A-7. When the activity from the nerve forces and the muscular plexus along any portion of the cerebrospinal system, from which organs or portions of the body receive their nerve impulse, are stimulated, this sets up a circulation that allows refuse forces or drosses from the system to be carried out in a normal way and manner. This is drainage, see? Not necessary that excesses only through the alimentary canal be increased in eliminations to make for proper drainage, but the muscular forces or tendons or bursae or the areas along the system where the nerve plexus produce the improper impulse need to be stimulated. This is why the activity through a massage properly osteopathically given sets up such drainages better than the administering of those things that stimulate an already disturbed condition between the deep circulation and the superficial, see (that is, through cathartics, etc., see)?

Hence these are the indications as we find for the body.

While it is necessary to stimulate the activity of the organs that are showing a tendency for slowness or laggardness in their activity, this must be done properly – from their impulses or centers along the cerebrospinal system – to be *effective* and to *maintain* an equilibrium. (E. C., 1140-1)

From this it is clear that stimulation of superficial and deep circulation is being avoided. Concentration is to the centers and ganglia along the spine that affect organs and plexuses allowing drainages to take place (see illustration 14).

Interestingly enough, all five persons had problems with eliminations and/or assimilations which is usually related to circulation, but none called for a massage to stimulate the circulation. When this is desirable, the massage is almost always down the spine.

Spinal massage towards the 9th dorsal is, I believe, also related to the use of the Wet Cell Appliance, for all five readings recommend its use. One of the primary purposes of the Wet Cell is to provide an electrical activity that energizes or stimulates a "force through the areas of the assimilating system, as from the lacteal duct plexus" (E. C., 2366-7), which is very near the umbilical plexus or solar plexus which is opposite the T_9 vertebra. Thus, the use of the Wet Cell encourages the flow of nerve impulses and energies into and through the solar plexus. Looking at a diagram of the autonomic nervous system (note: the autonomic is the combination of the sympathetic and parasympathetic systems; see Illustration 6), it is easy to see the relationship between the solar plexus and the abdominal organs of assimilation, elimination and the circulation in this area.

I think it is safe to deduce from this that massage toward the solar plexus stimulates the flow of nerve impulses not only to the ganglia of the brachial and lumbar plexuses along the spine, but towards the direction of the solar plexus. This is where energies enter the body and go directly to the lacteals[10] in the small intestine, which is a major area for assimilation.

COMMENCING FROM THE SOLAR PLEXUS

The third form of spinal massage begins in the middle of the spine at the 9th dorsal, the solar plexus area. Directions are usually given to massage gently in a circular motion along each side of the spine *from* the 9th dorsal to the base of the brain and out over the brachial plexuses, or downward *from* the 9th dorsal to the base of the spine and out over the lumbar and sacral plexuses. Sometimes the massage continues out the full length of nerve fibers on the arms and legs. (See illustration 13) The purpose of the massage is to stimulate nerve impulses of the autonomic nerve system, the cerebrospinal nerve system, and nerve fibers to coordinate and more easily convey their messages. Because there seems to be a relationship between this type of massage and the growth process of the body during and immediately following conception, one might maintain a sense of rebirthing during the massage.

I remember having a much too brief talk with Harvey Grady, Director of Research at the A.R.E. Clinic in Phoenix about the value of massage in the Edgar Cayce readings. At the time, I was just beginning my research for this book and was a little bit discouraged because I had not as yet gotten beyond the thousands of references to massage for the purpose of rubbing in various oils. Within a few weeks, however, I had found my way into the nervous system and the different kinds of massage I had been searching and hoping to find.

Grady suggested one fascinating subject that he believed would have to be considered when writing or lecturing about massage in the readings. And it was this that led me to the concept of "rebirthing" in massage. He referred to the series of readings given on the endocrine glands.[11] These readings were given to the Glad Helpers (the name of the Edgar Cayce Prayer Healing Group) during the years 1940 and 1941. They were seeking information to help understand "the functions of each of the seven major glandular centers in relation to other glands in the system, heredity, temperament, character, environment, physical, mental and spiritual growth and expression."[12]

For our purpose here, let me briefly describe Edgar Cayce's concept of the development of the endocrine glands, their functions and their relationship to massage, particularly to the unusual type of massage we're describing in this section (i.e., commencing from the solar plexus).

According to Cayce, at or some time after conception, the first development is that of the pituitary gland, the master gland of the body. Next is the pineal, which determines a person's individuality, size, shape, facial configuration, and so on. The third development is that of the umbilical cord which provides both a nutritional and mental connection to the mother. The fourth center to develop is the solar plexus glands, primarily the adrenals. These act "with the emotions and the growth and unfoldment of the body itself" (E.C., 281-47). These four developments all quite obviously occur very early in one's growth; in fact, within the first three weeks after conception (E.C., 281-47).

From the point of view of the Edgar Cayce readings, the glandular system has two functions: to help create a physical body and to create a physical connection with mental and spiritual forces: "Some of the activities of the glands relate to the purely physical functioning; yet the physical functioning in a life-giving body must of its very nature be empowered with mind and spirit" (E.C., 281-57).

This creative impulse reaches out from conception to first form the brain which is developed through the activites of the pineal gland. This is affected, according to Cayce, by the mind of the individual, its parents and its environment.

Next, the pineal-brain supplies what is needed for developing the physical body. "Ye know that it reverts then to the brain of the nervous system, to the solar plexus center, and then reflexes through its own MENTAL activity to the physical forces of the still developing body" (E.C., 281-57). This is very important to our study. Seven major glands (except the spleen) lie along the spinal cord and are activated by hormones, nerve impulses, and mental and spiritual impulses.

With this bit of background on the glands, the purpose of a massage commencing from the solar plexus down to the feet and upward and out to the hands suggests a parallel with how an individual comes into being from conception onward. It's almost as if the massage were trying to recreate and stimulate those impulses coming from the brain and going

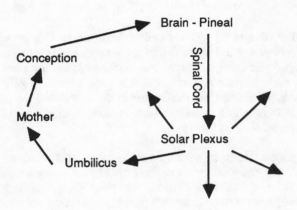

out from the solar plexus to coordinate with and help develop other parts of the body.

In a reading for a six-year-old boy born with a condition which made it difficult to grow strong and coordinated in both body and mind, the cause originated at the "...first impulse in those conditions existent from which this plasma came into physical experience" (E.C., 1146-1). Thus, at the very moment of conception, something went awry with the forces affecting the growth of the newborn. According to the Cayce readings, these forces are not only influenced in part by impulses containing mental desires, wishes, and hopes of the parents, but also those belonging to the soul of the one being conceived. For the soul is able to make choices concerning its development.

The reading for this child described the physical pathology as "adhesions in the umbilicus centers."

These, as we find, show a condition wherein there is *a stricture or an adherence to tissue* in same. Hence we have at times a violent reaction through the nerve forces in making their coordination in those areas to the centers along the cerebrospinal system in which the sympathetic or vegetative nerve system coordinates with the impulses for the various developments of the activity to the sensory system. (E.C., 1146-1, my emphasis)

For (this is not always understood), the various centers from which impulses to the activity of the sensory reactions receive their impulse arise from the pineal and the adrenals in their coordination with the plexus along the whole of the system itself. These become generated from the centers in the lacteal and the umbilicus plexus from which assimilations from food reactions to the system take place. (E.C., 1146-1)

Emphasis in treatment was to increase the effectiveness of communication or transmission of nerve impulses to the organs. Stimulation from the Wet Cell Appliance and massage were the two specific treatments recommended.

After each of these treatments [Wet Cell] there should be a *general easy massage from the central portion of the body to the tip of the toes, and from the 9th dorsal toward the head and to the tip of the fingers.* To be sure, make for associations with this connection in the *brachial plexus,* in the 1st and 2nd and 3rd cervical center or axis, and around the neck and through the vagus center extending to the lung forces themselves. (E.C., 1146-1, my emphasis)

This massage basically follows the pattern of fetal development. And because massage commencing from the solar plexus (9th dorsal) is not frequently recommended in the readings, its use suggests an attempt to not only stimulate the flow of nerve impulses through the nervous system to sensory organs, but possibly to stimulate the flow of mental forces or impulses to activate glands of the solar plexus and coordinate their activity with the brain – a rebirthing through the massage gently stimulating the nervous system to send its messages outward throughout the body.

The next case study applicable to massage commencing from the solar plexus is presented in a series of Cayce readings (372-1 through 372-8) given to a New York businessman over a four-year period. In addition, his business concerns provide us with some interesting business advice and information from the readings we might not have accessed otherwise.

The man owned two businesses, a shoe store and a real estate office. The shoe store worried him, for business had fallen off 50% within the last year, the lease to the property was expiring, the building needed alterations, and the two men running the store weren't doing very well to promote the business of selling shoes. He wondered whether he should sell or expand. In response, the reading suggested he renew the lease and ask the landlord for financial help to remodel. He was told not to expand to another location and to reserve selling the business until a more opportune time. He was also advised to replace the men running the store and to advertise, for "Advertising pays in any direction."[13] In regard to the real estate business, he was advised not to stress himself in too many activities and to take in partners. Overwork, financial distress, and worry had set the stage for a classic case of stress.

Along with his business concerns, it was severe pain, especially at night, that prompted his first readings. He would have so much discomfort in his heart region and in his back that he couldn't sleep. His readings indicated that the pain was due to gas pressure pushing up on the second cardiac plexus and poor circulation. Digestion, especially as it relates to the functions of the pancreas and liver, was adversely affected by adhesions around the 5th and 6th dorsals and overeating. This resulted in toxicity which then affected movement of his limbs. Use of an electric vibrator along the spine before sleep was suggested to help relax him. Otherwise, treatment was fairly simple: a "prescription" to aid assimilation, change in diet, and enemas. But the most important advice concerned his mental attitude: "Worrying only brings for self detrimental conditions, and very seldom – if ever – aids in meeting conditions better, but rather unfits one for the *stress* as is brought to bear" (E.C., 372-2, my italics). Had he been able to reverse the trend set in motion by worry, perhaps what happened over the next few years would not have resulted.

The information in the readings indicates that on January 13, 1930, he entered the Cayce Hospital in Virginia Beach with "autointoxication and chronic stomach trouble." Over the next five days he received vapor baths, salt glow massage (salt moistened with water), rubdowns with witch hazel, manipulation, and some minor osteopathic adjustments.

Three months later, he is told that conditions for a stroke are being set up; his physician has already prescribed digitalis. Just getting out of bed is now difficult.

His condition continued to deteriorate over the next three years. His seventh reading lists his complaints as headaches, indigestion, nausea, tingling or trembling in extremities, and a general incoordination within his body. The suggestions for treatment remained pretty much the same as those previously given except for the massage. Why he continued to seek Cayce's advice when he rarely followed it is a mystery. However, here is the new massage recommendation relative to the third major pattern of neuromassage.

...massage along the cerebro-spinal system, *commencing from the solar plexus center and rubbing down and then from the solar plexus center and rubbing up* – not commencing up at the head and rubbing all the way down, not commencing at the bottom and rubbing all the way up; *but from the centers towards the locomotaries of the lower portion of body,* as much as the body will absorb of this combination:

To 2 ounces of rub alcohol, add:

Russian White Oil, 1 ounce,

Witch hazel, 1 ounce,

Oil of Sassafras, 1/4 ounce.

This, when massaged along the spine, will tend to make for *a better superficial coordination in nerve and blood supply impulse from the centers in the cerebro-spinal system.* In this rub, particular attention should be given to the solar plexus, the lumbar plexus, the brachial plexus – see? (E.C., 372-7, my emphasis)

This was a specific massage to meet his condition at the time. The primary emphasis here is threefold: 1) to massage into the ganglia along the spine a stimulating combination of oils; 2) to stimulate the superficial circulation away from the heart toward the hands and feet; and 3) to stimulate the brachial, lumbar, and solar plexus. The significance of 2) and 3) is best explained in another reading:

Then, to meet these would be to have those of the manipulation and *masseur* in the way and manner that the whole body may receive the proper relaxation for the full even flow of the bloodstream through the system. Now get this! Not as has *been* received by the body, but in the way and manner that all centers of the cerebrospinal and sympathetic system that form plexus of functioning with the various organs of the body may be so relaxed that the bloodstream may flow through same in a manner that will bring coordination of the impulse from such radiating centers. (E.C., 88-1)

Manipulation and massage of the sympathetic nervous system's nerve centers along the spine and of the plexuses formed by spinal nerves coming from the cerebrospinal nervous system (brachial and lumbar plexuses) can thus increase blood flow to and through these areas.

On October 10, 1933, he received his last reading. The reading said the changes in his body were ominous; he was slowly dying. He was tired and without hope; his strength was diminishing; he couldn't keep his food down; enemas were needed regularly; his legs were swelling and painful; there was a buzzing in his ears; he was losing weight and unable to put it back on; he had stomach pains and cirrhosis of the liver. His doctors diagnosed the condition as cancer, but the reading said not yet, but it could become that.

Treatment changed a little with the addition of "deep therapy in the electrical vibrations" (diathermy) immediately followed with a massage along the spine with olive oil and myrrh.

Q-8. How often should the olive oil and tincture of myrrh be applied?

A-8. As indicated, the massage of these properties into the spine should be applied particularly soon after the use of the deep therapy machine. For, while there is the activity of the electrical forces in the body, the ganglia along the spine will respond to the necessary forces for absorption better than when there is less electrical force in the body, see? Hence, these massages would be given in this manner, for the activity of such would be as this:

The oil, as it were, is to relax the tendencies for contraction through impulses that are lacking, as indicated, or that are excessive (for both occur), in the ganglia of the cerebro-spinal system.

The myrrh, as an activative force with the oil, acts as a healing influence to the tendency of inflammation or *drying* of the texture or tendril effect of muscular activities of the system. (E.C., 372-8)

Actually, it is the important information on the value of olive oil and myrrh in the reading that first interested me. And much too frequently, this is all we come away with from a reading – a little bit of valuable information about an oil, a massage, or a hydrotherapy. What we miss is the story, the context of the information. For here is the story of a man in his 50s, having been under a great deal of stress and tension, and now nearing the end of his life. During all of this, he is receiving help from his family, physicians, and Edgar Cayce, and eventually sharing with all of us the information in his readings. Although he died at the age of 58 on New Year's Eve 1933, there is much in his readings which may help us not only in the applications of massage and oils, but in illustrating how deeply our mental attitudes affect our body, especially through the solar plexus: that area which is symbolic of what we digest, physically, mentally, and spiritually, all that comes to us both from within and without.

UP THE SPINE – UPWARD

Of the approximate 1,700 readings catalogued under "Nervous System: Incoordination" (referring to incoordination between the cerebrospinal and sympathetic nervous sytems), I have found only three readings which call for massage up the spine toward the brain. (The majority, as indicated earlier, recommend massage *down the spine*. That is, a gentle circular massage along the spine over the erector spinae *from* the base of the brain to the base of the spine using the fingertips.) In the Cayce readings, recommendation for massage up the spine is restricted to very specific conditions where massage must be given with great sensitivity for painful physical symptoms and/or mental distress.

The first reading was given for a 38-year-old woman who described these symptoms: neck and backaches, nose and throat problems, a weak stomach, a breaking out on the face and possible indications of pyorrhea. In addition, she was tired and seemed bewildered and unable to concentrate at times. "Why am I so nervous?" she asked Cayce.

The reading described her condition as basically a glandular problem affecting the circulation, nervous system, and organs. Poor eliminations had resulted from organs affected by the glands involved. Apparently, the situation was critical enough to require treatments which didn't provide too much stimulation:

First there must be the setting up of eliminations through the alimentary canal in such a way and manner as not to produce irritation to the lower or the upper hepatic circulation, not to overexcite the heart's activity, not to produce too great a strain but to bring coordination to most of the organs in their relationships to proper activity of their bodily functionings. (E. C., 513-2)

Further treatment included a tonic, a laxative, the Radio-Active Appliance, rest, oil, massage, and dietary advice.

Have an oil massage (this may be begun almost immediately) each evening with an equal combination of Olive Oil, Tincture of Myrrh, Compound Tincture of Benzoin. Heat the Olive Oil to add the Myrrh and the Benzoin; not to boiling, but so they will mix together. *Massage this combination especially in the joints of the body; knees, feet, across the hips, up the spine – upward..* Massage gently all the body will absorb. (E. C., 513-2)

Gentle massage up the spine tends to emphasize afferent (toward the brain and spinal cord) nerve flow thereby putting less stress on efferent (away from the brain and spinal cord) nerve impulses going to the upper and lower hepatic circulation and the heart. Also, this is an *oil massage*, meaning the olive oil, Tincture of Myrrh and Benzoin help stimulate eliminations in a milder and less irritating manner than a general body massage. Thus, the combination of massage up the spine with a specific oil mixture provides gentle stimulation to the spine (and the joints).

The second reading was given for a 27-year-old man diagnosed by his doctor as having "acute mania." Since the age of ten or eleven he had experienced several nervous breakdowns. Physically, his major difficulty was walking.

From Cayce's remarkable viewpoint, the reading described birth injuries as the original cause of "a lesion that pulsates" somewhere between the 12th dorsal and the 4th lumbar "in the nervous system itself." The result was an incoordination between "that cord called the pineal with its coordination with the adrenal and the lacteal plexus" from pressures on the nerves. The boy was characterized as "constantly under a nerve strain."

Treatment consisted of hot castor oil packs, the Radio-Active Appliance, dietary suggestions, osteopathy, and spinal massage from the coccyx to the 9th dorsal and sometimes the base of the brain.

And following same (each day after the Pack is given), have a general and gentle massage from the coccyx, specifically, to the 9th dorsal, and occasionally (once or twice a week) coordinating the rest of the cerebrospinal centers with same. But each day the Pack is given, massage the lower portion of the spine gently in a neuropathic manner, circular on either side of the spine, holding the centers especially in the coccyx end of the spine itself. And after these are given for four to five periods, gradually make a *correction* of the *end* of the coccyx bone itself, *as* the body is the more thoroughly relaxed. (E. C., 1168-1)

In answer to a question at the end of the reading, Cayce makes it clear that the young man's condition is not acute mania and that the purpose of the treatments is to relieve pressures on the glands by breaking up the lesion. This would provide a stimulus to restore proper glandular functioning in terms of coordination between the brain and the sensory system.

The third reading, 4885-1, was given for a woman with hypertension and ulcers in the duodenum which affected the condition of her entire body. Due to the severity of her pain and critical condition, a gentle massage "from the sacrum to the cervicals" was recommended. This would provide minimal stimulation to the body while allowing the massage to aid absorption of an herbal prescription she was to take. (She was also directed to drink lots of water). Gently, slowly and naturally, the body would thus be brought back into balance.

Though the following reading does not illustrate massage *up the spine*, it is a very interesting variation of spinal massage. Interesting because relaxation of the lower spine, and I'm speaking of the coccyx area only, produces an effect on the "centers at the base of the brain." It is a response of the cerebrospinal and sympathetic nervous systems to the release of pressures on the nerves in the coccygeal area. Let's take a look at this case.

A young woman, 23 years of age, was having difficulty with shortness of breath, tingling sensations throughout her body, coldness and numbness in parts of her extremities, headaches often followed by nausea, and a tightness across the shoulders and the base of the brain. There was also swelling near the thyroid and a hemorrhoid condition. Like so many other cases we have seen, Cayce traced the cause of these conditions to incoordination between the cerebrospinal and sympathetic nervous systems. In this case, an injury earlier in her life caused the problem.

These conditions then, as we find, have to do primarily with pressures which exist in the cerebrospinal system, and the effect is more specific to the sympathetic or vegetative nerve forces.

We find that these exist from an injury which happened some time ago, and is to the end of the spine. This pressure upon the nerves through the coccyx area of the end of the spine causes the contraction in the centers at the base of the brain; and the pressure upon the medulla oblongata – which is that equalizing center between the cerebrospinal and the sympathetic system, as it enters the base of the brain – causes the lack of the flow of blood and of impulse to portions of the body. (E. C., 2130-1)

Treatment included osteopathy, wet heat, electrical treatments, and Atomidine for the thyroid. If the acute disturbances returned, Cayce said to "massage the sacral and the coccyx area, or close to the end of the spine, with plain table salt saturated with pure apple vinegar; then apply an electric pad or the like. This will relieve tension" (E.C., 2130-1).

Endnotes:

[1] See Wm. A. McGarey, M.D., "Muscular Dystrophy," *Physician's Reference Notebook*, (Virginia Beach, VA: A.R.E. Press, 1983).

[2] Ibid.

[3] Irvin Korr, D.O., "The Sympathetic Nervous System as Mediator Between the Somatic and Supportive Processes," *The Collected Papers of Irvin M. Korr* (Colorado Springs, CO: American Academy of Osteopathy, 1979).

[4] Irvin Korr, D.O., "The Spinal Cord as Organizer of Disease Processes: The Peripheral Autonomic Nervous System," *The Collected Papers of Irvin M. Korr* (Colorado Springs, CO: American Academy of Osteopathy, 1979).

[5] Stupes are flannel or other cloths soaked in hot liquid (water, turpentine, etc.) and applied to the skin as a counterirritant (fomentation).

[6] I would also recommend Phil Nuernberger, Ph.D., *Freedom From Stress* (Honesdale, PA: Himalayan International Institute of Yoga Science and Philosophy, 1981).

[7] Ibid. Dr. Nuernberger highly recommends biofeedback as an important tool in learning and understanding about stress

in our lives. A biofeedback "instrument acts like a mirror, giving one immediate information about what is happening inside his body." With this information we can then learn to control our mental and physical impulses so that they don't create bodily or psychological dysfunction.

[8] Wet Cell Appliance. See next endnote.

[9] The Wet Cell Appliance is an electrical device often recommended in the readings, approximately 975 times. It produces a very small electrical current. See *Edgar Cayce Encyclopedia of Healing*, p. 520 ff.

[10] Lacteals: "That portion that makes for the ability of the system to take from the food values and prepare same in the manner in which same may be used to revivify, revitalize, recharge the system itself" (E. C.,1055-1).

According to Dr. McGarey, the lacteals in the Edgar Cayce readings are "not only the villi of the small intestine, but also the single lymph nodules and the Peyer's patches found in the small intestinal wall, the collecting lymphatics, and the lymph nodes found along the way, through which the lymph passes. This would be contrary to the conventional concept of lacteals found in the field of physiology" (*Palma Christi*, p.20).

[11] See 281-46 ff. in "Meditation, Part I: Healing Prayer and The Revelation," *The Library Series*, Vol. 2, (Virginia Beach, VA: Edgar Cayce Foundation, 1974).

[12] Ibid, p.234

[13] Quoted from one of his son's readings, 417-4.

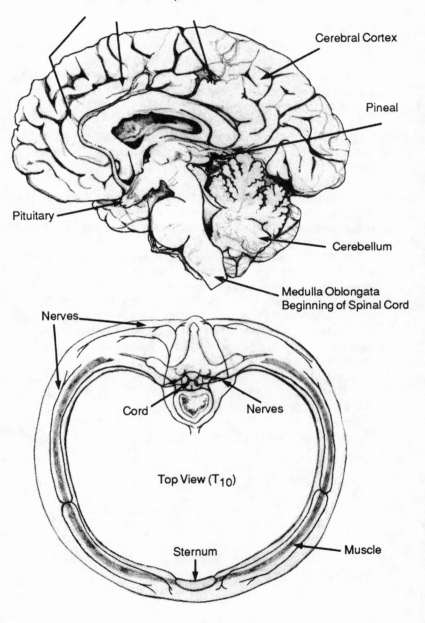

Illust. #1 – The Brain
Illust. #3 – Cross Section of Spine & Body Cavity (at T₁₀)

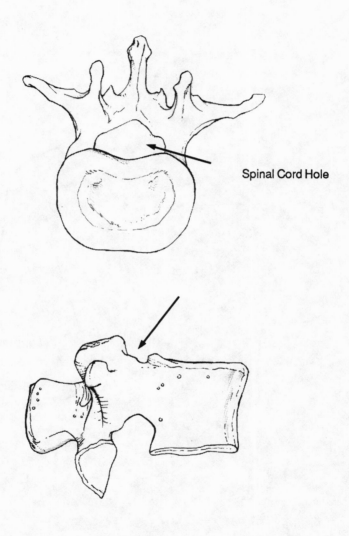

Spinal Cord Hole

Illust. #2 – Two Views of a Vertebra (top & side)

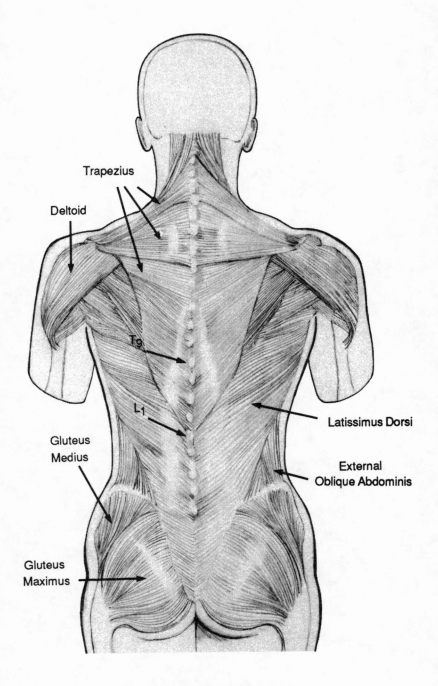

Illust. #4 – Back Muscles

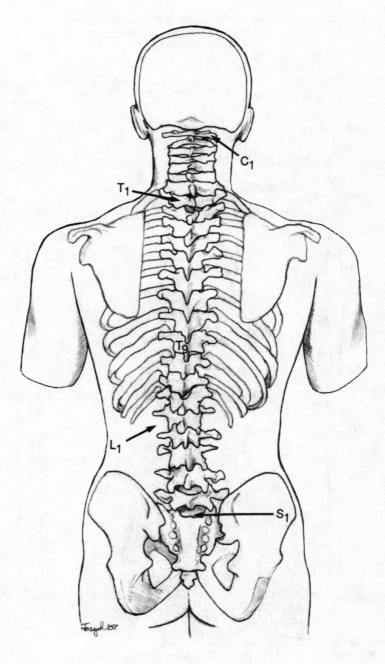

Illust. #5 – Back Bones

Illust. #6 – Sympathetic & Parasympathetic System with Ganglia and Plexuses.

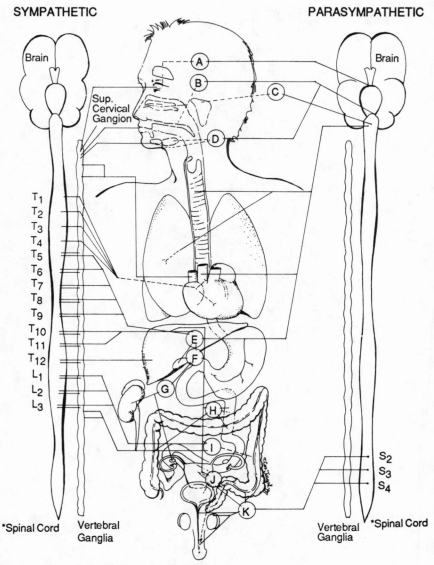

SYMPATHETIC

PARASYMPATHETIC

Brain

Brain

Sup. Cervical Ganglion

(A)

(B)

(C)

(D)

T₁
T₂
T₃
T₄
T₅
T₆
T₇
T₈
T₉
T₁₀
T₁₁
T₁₂
L₁
L₂
L₃

(E)
(F)
(G)
(H)
(I)
(J)
(K)

S₂
S₃
S₄

*Spinal Cord   Vertebral Ganglia

Vertebral Ganglia   *Spinal Cord

*Note: Spinal Cord technically ends between L₂ & L₃, but the Sympathetic & ParaSympathetic Continues on to the tailbone.

A – Ciliary Ganglion, B – Sphenopalatine Ganglion, C – Optic Ganglion,
D – Submandibular Ganglion, E & F – Celiac Plexus, G – Renal Plexus,
H – Inf. Mesenteric Plexus, I – Hypogastric Plexus, J – Aortic Plexus,
K – Plevic Plexus.

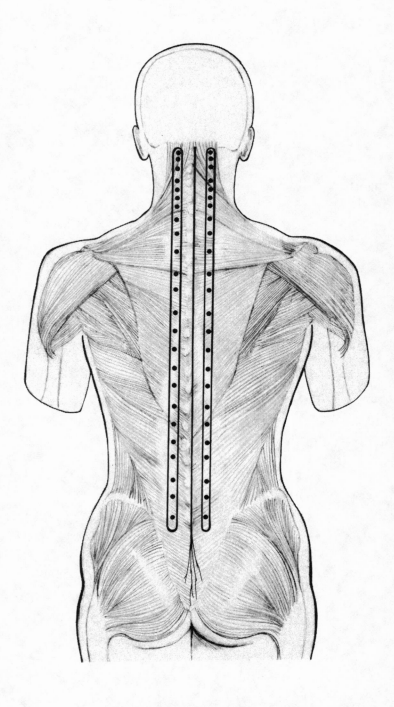

Illust. #7 – Cerebrospinal & Sympathetic Nerves

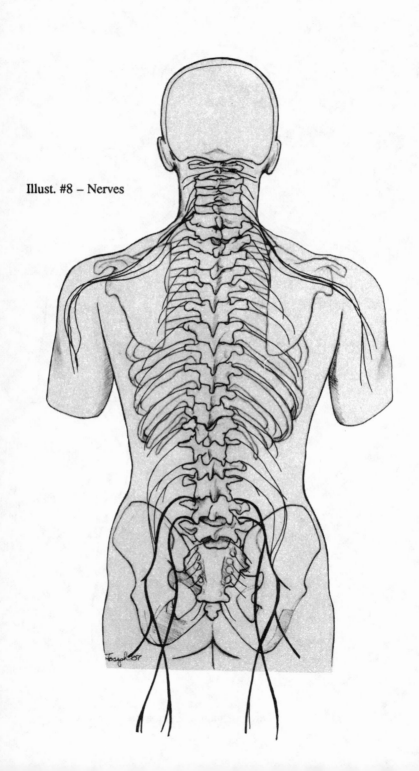

Illust. #8 – Nerves

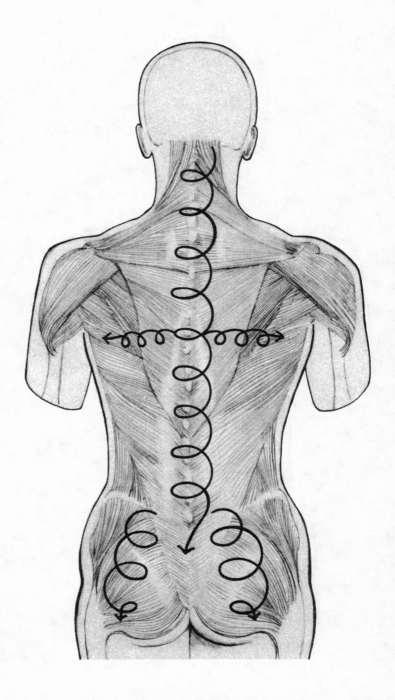

Illust. #9 – Circular Massage Down the Spine

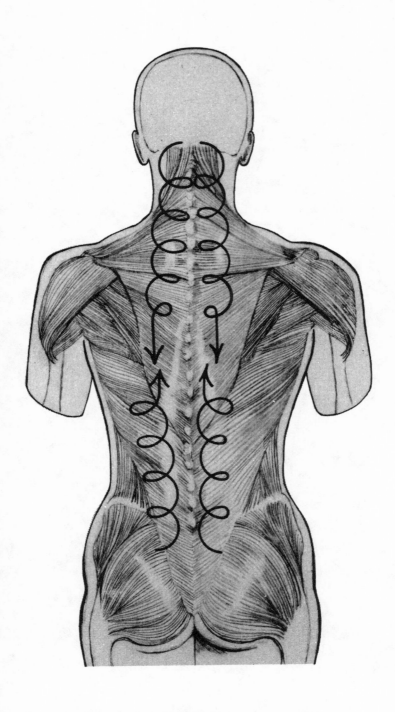

Illust. #10 – Circular Massage Toward T9

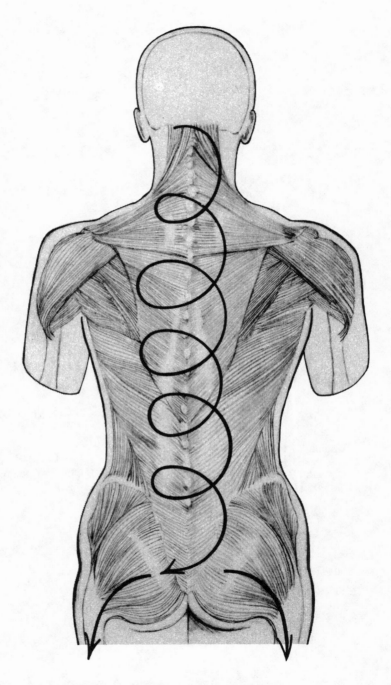

Illust. #11 – Circular Massage Down the Spine

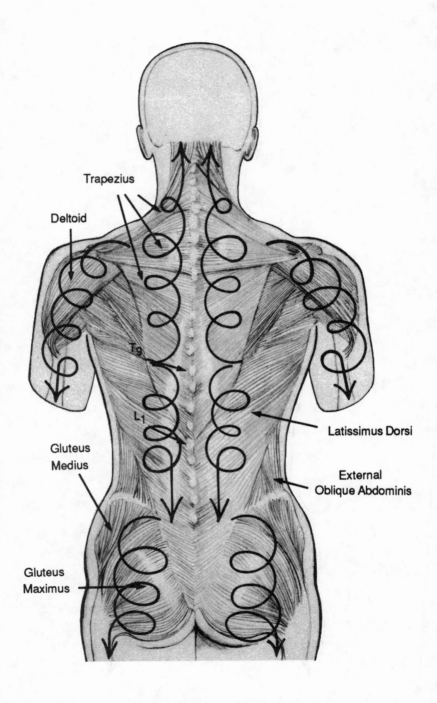

Illust. #12 – Massage away from T$_9$

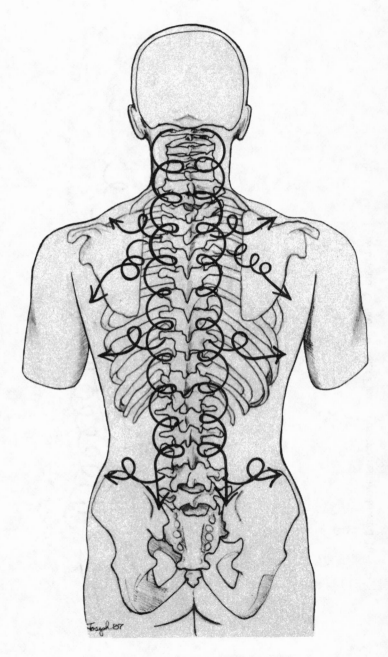

Illust. #13 – Massage Down and Out

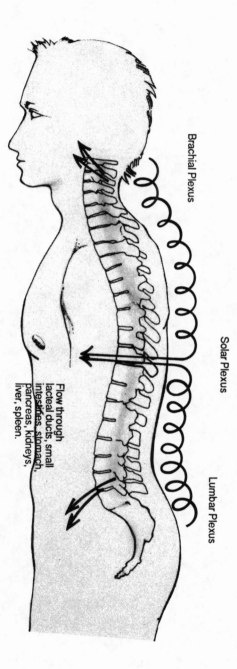

Brachial Plexus

Solar Plexus

Lumbar Plexus

Flow through
lacteal ducts, small
intestines, stomach,
pancreas, kidneys,
liver, spleen.

Illust. #14 – Flow toward & through Solar Plexus during massage toward T9

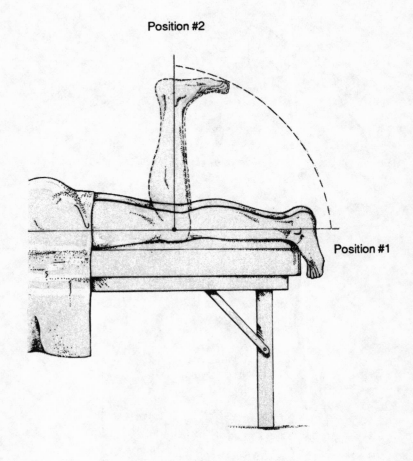

Position #2

Position #1

Illust. #15 – Short Leg Measurement Positions 1 & 2

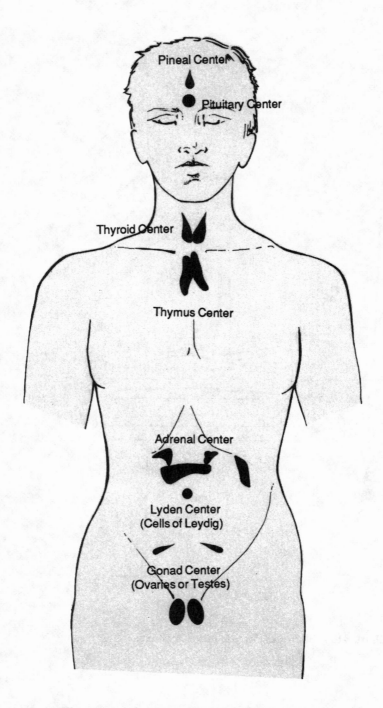

Illust. #16 – Endocrine Glands, Spiritual Centers

Chapter Five

SHORT LEG TECHNIQUE PLEXUSES & CHAKRAS

A few years ago, a young high school basketball player came to my office with a pulled hamstring in her right leg. She had seen a physician who recommended rest and massage. The youngster was in some pain and limping. There was a little edema around the lower hamstring but no bruising. I used castor oil packs, massage, and strengthening exercises for the affected leg and within a few days she was back on the court with a support bandage.

This isn't an unusual story except for one thing. I always check a person's leg length to help me determine the major area of muscular tension and contraction when there is a complaint or injury. In this case, examination revealed a short leg pattern relating to the left side of the neck! Palpation of the neck muscles indeed revealed deep soreness and contraction, a situation that may have existed for a long time but without any noticeable irritation.

Going back to her immediate problem, I explained to her that with a short left leg, the muscles on her right side would tend to stretch a little to compensate for the muscular tension and contraction on the left side, making that leg short.[1] In effect, the hamstrings in the right leg were stretched or pulled before the injury but not enough to cause a problem. Filling me in on the activities leading up to her injury, she said her basketball coach had held two practices that day, one in the afternoon and a second in the evening. He wanted a winning team and was pushing a little too much with a second practice. The youngster was fatigued, but also trying to give more than 100%! In that situation, the chronically stretched hamstring pulled, a slight micro-tear possibly, resulting in pain and limping. Normally, this would never have happened, but given a short left leg, a tendency for the right side to be slightly stretched or pulled, and over-exertion, the muscle gave in and she had a "pulled muscle."

After working on her leg, I began to massage her neck.

She had not been aware of the tightness here. In fact, she had no idea how it had gotten that way, recalling no earlier injury or fall, but she did remember that for about a year of her life she couldn't walk. Her parents had had to carry her. Doctors could find nothing to solve the mystery.

Going further back in time, she spoke of her mother's becoming very ill and having to be hospitalized for several weeks. The child was just two years old then. The mother became mentally ill and continued to be hospitalized off and on over a period of years. It's obvious from this very brief family history that the girl grew up in an emotionally difficult situation. Psychologically, there was much to give her a "pain in the neck."

Tension, anxiety, emotion, and life situations play a significant role in sustained muscular contraction.[2] At the age of 16, the condition usually hasn't developed into a disabling backache or migraine headache, but in this case, a musculoskeletal pattern was developing and creating a stress or a condition of muscular tension in the pulled or stretched muscles so that their capability or threshold to maintain their integrity was greatly diminished. Excess fatigue and use were the straw that broke the camel's back.

My advice to the youngster was to begin strengthening exercises for her right hamstrings,[3] to begin relaxing and stretching the left side of her neck, and to try to understand the underlying emotional reasons for the tension here. Hopefully, she could then work through them and release her hold on them.

The significance of this story is in illustrating how valuable it is to know where to give massage. Massage therapists are educated and trained to determine which muscles are tense and contracted. But had I treated the hamstring only, I feel certain it would have been of temporary value. A future injury in the same area was highly probable, especially assuming that the musculoskeletal system would remain out of balance. The use of the short leg technique, however, directed me to treatment of the neck, which facilitated the coordination of the full musculoskeletal system. Let me explain.

Muscles almost always work in groups, movement is a

coordinated action of several muscles. Furthermore, when one or more muscles contract, there is usually a reciprocal response of relaxation or stretching in its opposite muscle group. It's not difficult to see that if a group of muscles such as those rotating a leg or laterally flexing the neck contract and stay that way, those muscles in the opposite hip or side of the neck will also remain stretched in order to compensate for the contraction. The client will usually complain of pain on the stretched side.

Let's see what the short leg technique is and what it can tell us. The client should lie face down on the table with arms at the side. The head should be straight, and not turned to the left or the right. The bottom of the heels should be viewed in two positions: 1) prone and 2) at a 90° angle to the table (see illustration 15). Make sure the body is straight, the legs parallel, and then observe the length at the heels. Second, while holding the feet together, lift the legs together to 90° and check the heels again, making sure the soles of the feet are approximately parallel with the table. These two positions can reveal muscular tension and contraction, as well as indicate where they are by the pull of the body to the left or right.

When one leg is short, that side of the body usually has the most muscular tension and contraction. This has to be taken into consideration in any program of massage and exercise.

Next, there are five significant patterns in the short leg technique. These patterns reveal muscular tension and contraction either on the left or right side of the body in the 1) neck, 2) shoulder, 3) low back, 4) hip (pelvic), and 5) below the waist but not in the pelvic area.

1) Neck: If the same leg is short in both position 1 and 2, the muscles in the side of the neck on the short leg side are in tension and contraction.

2) Shoulder: If one leg is short in position 1, but becomes even in position 2, then the area of contraction is between the neck and the waist (usually the shoulder) on the side of the short leg.

3) Low back: If the legs are even in position 1, but one

becomes shorter in position 2, then the area of contraction is in the low back (lumbar area) on the side of the short leg.

4) Hip (pelvic): If one leg is short in position 1, but becomes longer in position 2, then the area of contraction is in the hip or pelvis on the side of the short leg in position 1.

5) Below the waist (but not in the pelvic area): If the legs are even in position 1, and one becomes longer in position 2, then the area of contraction is between the waist and the foot on the side of the short leg, excluding the pelvic area.

Patterns 3 and 5 may appear difficult to assess at first, but after a number of observations the movement of the leg will become clear.

THE USE OF LEG LENGTH TO DETERMINE AREAS OF CONTRACTION

Prone on table with arms at side, head face down, legs parallel.

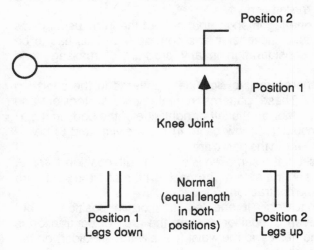

Position 2

Position 1

Knee Joint

Position 1
Legs down

Normal
(equal length
in both
positions)

Position 2
Legs up

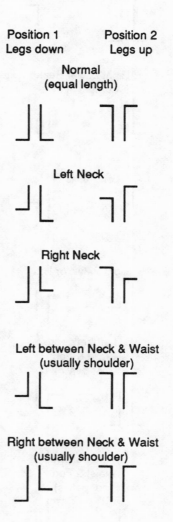

Position 1
Legs down

Position 2
Legs up

Normal
(equal length)

Left Neck

Right Neck

Left between Neck & Waist
(usually shoulder)

Right between Neck & Waist
(usually shoulder)

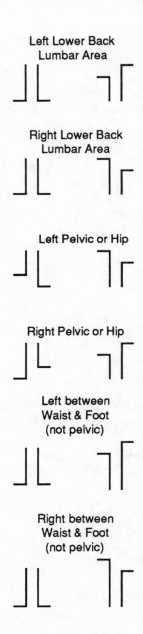

Left Lower Back
Lumbar Area

Right Lower Back
Lumbar Area

Left Pelvic or Hip

Right Pelvic or Hip

Left between
Waist & Foot
(not pelvic)

Right between
Waist & Foot
(not pelvic)

Let me share another example of this concept in actual practice. The owner of a Nautilus Center came to me for a massage because he couldn't turn his head due to neck pain. His head was slightly flexed to his right side, movement without pain on the left side of his neck was extremely difficult, and he hadn't been able to look behind when driving for several years.

The short leg technique revealed a short right leg in positions 1 and 2. (See "Neck" under the five significant patterns in the short leg technique.) Therefore, the muscles in the right side of his neck were contracted and needed relaxing. The lateral flexor muscles on the left side of his neck needed strengthening, for they were being pulled and stretched, causing severe pain. One session of heat and massage helped him immensely. Also during the session, he told me that he had been trying to help himself by working out on the neck machine at Nautilus. He kept strengthening the right side of his neck because the left hurt so much! A quick reverse in the use of weights changed his life. He soon was able to see behind and to the side when driving.

This is a simple example. What's not so simple is when people come to me almost as a last resort. They have been to traditional health professionals where physical exams have already ruled out any physical cause; they may have received treatment at the pain site. But inevitably, the short leg technique reveals a primary pattern opposite the area of pain. For example, I frequently see people with chronic low backpain.[4] They've already gone the traditional route and are willing by now to try anything – even massage. Quite often the short leg technique reveals muscular contraction in the pelvic area, left or right. (The complaint of pain in the lumbar area or low back is almost always on the opposite side of the pelvic contraction.) Usually the contraction is in the gluteals and the rotators, especially the piriformis. Heat and deep massage help relax the muscles and tendons of the hip and at the same time relieve the strain or pulling in the erector spinae group.

This is the kind of work I've been doing for years. I've trained myself to trust the short leg information and not to be

115

misled by the site of the pain, though attention must be given here, especially in breaking down adhesions and strengthening the pulled muscles. I have to admit that the short leg method doesn't solve every problem; for example, it doesn't help with bilateral contraction. And there are also occasions when a person should be referred to other health care professionals. But when its use is valid, the advantages are numerous. Let me tell you about them.

Of major value is that it assists the massage practitioner in immediately determining primary and secondary areas of muscular tension and contraction that may be causing strain and distortion to posture. An added benefit is being able to identify which muscle or muscle groups are being pulled, strained, or stretched (another form of tension created by the pain of a pulled muscle). Once the first pattern is resolved, it may even reveal a second and third pattern.

Having thus made a diagnosis, a treatment plan can be formulated and effective therapy initiated during the very first session. The resulting benefits to the client are many. Alleviation or cessation of pain and healing occur sooner so that fewer sessions are required for treatment. Fewer sessions translates to money in the client's pocket because it reduces treatment expenditures and allows the client to return to the work place or resume his or her normal life sooner.

The short leg technique not only leads to areas of muscle contraction, but to major plexuses in the body as well as the paravertebral muscles related to these plexuses. For example, if a short leg pattern reveals muscular tension and contraction between the neck and waist on the right side, it is highly probable that the brachial plexus is involved. Therefore, it would be prudent to assess all the muscles related to this plexus. Massage therapists often see persons with arm pain and limited range of motion, yet no pathology has been detected through x-rays and medical examinations. If it's a muscular problem, the massage therapist is in a good position to help the person learn to relax and regain mobility of the arm. Assuming the short leg pattern matches the complaint, work can begin immediately in that area.[5] And hopefully the person can begin to understand his physical problem in relation to his emotions and mental attitudes.

The word "plexus" comes from a Latin word meaning *braid*. It refers to a network of nerves or blood vessels, a place where they come very close together. In fact, according to Cayce, this is where the association between the cerebrospinal and sympathetic nervous systems is closest. For example, reading 4054-1 says:

When the massages are given, especially after a warm bath, massage the areas particularly in the secondary cardiac plexus or the brachial plexus the 9th dorsal and the lumbar axis. Stimulate these areas with the oil massages. These massages may be done by a masseur or an osteopath. Such treatments should be of a relaxing nature, not stimulating in corrections; supplying to those centers particularly where there is the closer association with sympathetic nervous system and the cerebrospinal system. (E.C., 4054-1)

There are six major plexuses along the spine, all frequently referred to in the Cayce readings: cervical (neck), brachial (shoulder), cardiac (heart), solar or celiac (stomach), lumbar (low back), and sacral (deep in the pelvic cavity and anterior to the piriformis muscle). It is from these centers along the spinal cord that spinal nerves branch out, subdivide and form intricate and complex networks or patterns which eventually supply nerve fibers to the skeletal muscles and skin of our arms, legs, and abdomen.

To illustrate, let me describe two of these plexuses: the cardiac and the solar plexuses (or celiac plexus). The former is made up of autonomic nerve fibers and located very near the arch of the aorta. Sympathetic nerve fibers supplying the heart leave the ganglia located next to the first four thoracic vertebrae (T_1 - T_4) to form the cardiac plexus. The latter is associated with the 9th and 10th thoracic vertebrae. Sympathetic nerve fibers from ganglia near these vertebrae join and form the celiac (from the Greek word meaning *belly*) plexus, and from here branch out and supply abdominal viscera.

It's not hard to see that when muscles in the neck,

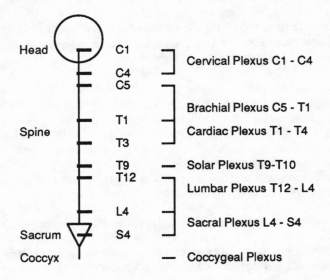

Note: The Thoracic nerves extend from T1 through T12, the Lumbar nerves from L1 through L5, and the Sacral nerves from S1 through S5.

Also see illustrations 5, 6, 7, & 8 in the center of this book.

shoulder, low back, hip, or abdomen become tense, spastic, or contracted, this can adversely affect the flow of blood, lymph, and nerve impulses through these plexuses. If the condition becomes chronic, then the muscle, in effect, actually resists relaxation. Proprioceptors, the deep sensory organs in the muscle, send impulses relaying information about position, motion, and tension back to the spinal cord, and a vicious cycle may be set up keeping the muscle contracted with body posture affected.[6]

As is pointed out over and over again in the Cayce readings, this type of situation can reflex not only back to the central nervous system, but also to the sympathetic nervous system. Lack of coordination between the two results. Consequently, the sympathetic nervous system as mediator between the musculoskeletal system, the viscera, and the mind is unable to bring into harmony the different parts and functions of the body and mind.

The body and mind relationship is the subject of a comprehensive book, *Bodymind*, by Ken Dychtwald, Ph.D. Anyone practicing massage would find it an invaluable resource, for it illustrates how personal growth, character, physical structure, dis-ease, and illness are intimately related to each other. The treatment of someone with an arm problem, like the example mentioned earlier, might well be enhanced by reading and understanding excerpts like this: "The shoulders, arms, hands, and upper back are primarily involved with the 'doing' and 'expressing' aspects of one's character. Through observing their form and function, we can learn quite a bit about the way a person handles himself in the world."[7]

Knowledge that the specific areas of greater coordination along the spine relate to plexuses adds a greater mental dimension to massage. And when one realizes that the plexuses are related to specific chakras, as well, we have added the spiritual dimension. "Chakra" comes from a sanskrit word meaning "wheel of energy." In ancient Hindu literature there are seven major energy centers or chakras in the body. Each represents specific aspects of human behavior and development, and each is related to a specific point along the spine. According to the Edgar Cayce readings, these chakras are associated with the endocrine glands (see illustration 16). In Kundalini yoga, there is a hollow channel or canal inside the spine. Along this canal, from the base of the torso (the Root Chakra) to the top of the head (the Crown Chakra) flows the Kundalini energy – the most powerful energy of all. This kundalini energy may well be the "elan vital" of Western thought. When released, it flows through each chakra. Each center represents a portion of the yogi's psychoemotional development.

There are some variations on the location of each chakra and the path the kundalini follows, but here are descriptions according to the Cayce readings and some Eastern texts. It is with the Eastern texts that some of the following information differs. For example, the Crown chakra is often considered the highest in Eastern teachings, but Cayce considers the Third Eye highest.

The first chakra is related to survival needs – basic material and primitive needs. It is called the Root Chakra, where the "serpent" lies coiled for action. Its color is red; its element, earth; its astrological influence, Saturn. From out of this center comes raw energy, unguided. It is associated with the genitals (Cayce says, "Gonads") and procreation, but procreation from urge rather than love. When this energy is guided by a higher ideal than the self-gratification of basic urges, it becomes a powerful component in the harmony and strength of the whole system – body, mind and spirit. If this center is blocked, then the characteristics so common to sexual repression become evident. Left unguided, flowing wherever the urge leads, it drains the system of its vital energy, and life gives way to death. In either case, the balance is lost; dis-ease results.

At the second chakra, our concerns are primarily interpersonal relationships, especially those generated by sexuality. Its color is orange; its astrological influence, Neptune; its element, water. According to ancient Tibetan teachings, it is located "three fingers below the navel," and called the Lower Abdomen Chakra, the pelvic plexus (L_1-S_4). Cayce identifies it with the Cells of Leydig and describes it as the mystical "seat of the soul," where it lies encased in matter. When a higher ideal begins to guide the Kundalini, the soul is freed. However, when this center is blocked, creativity diminishes and, like the first chakra, signs of repressed sexual energy become evident. In some mysterious way, this center also affects the imagination. Cayce says it has a direct link to the Crown chakra.

As the first two levels of needs are met or guided by a higher purpose, the third chakra, the powerful solar plexus (T_9-T_{10}), begins to expand or focus energy toward a larger world of power, ambition, ego and control. Its color is yellow; its element, fire; its astrological influence, Mars. According to Cayce, this center does not just generate energy, but, as an electrical transformer, it takes the kundalini energy from other centers giving it more impulse to move. Once again, where it moves depends on the ideals and purposes of the individual. As you might expect, Cayce identifies this center with the powerful adrenal glands.

If the third chakra is unguided, the energy can either turn outward and attempt to overpower and control everyone and everything, or it can turn inward and completely overwhelm a person. In *Myths to Live By*, Joseph Campbell writes about what happens to the Kundalini energy (or "serpent power") when it is selfishly guided or loosened at this level. He says, "the governing interest of anyone whose unfolding serpent power has become established on this plane is in consuming, conquering, turning all into his own substance, or forcing all to conform to his way of thought" (p. 111).

The fourth chakra, the Heart Center, is located in the center of the chest. Cayce identifies it with the Thymus gland. Its color is green; its astrological influence, Venus; its element, air. This chakra is associated with the Cardiac plexus (T_1-T_4). When it's in balance and flowing, love lives with vitality; it is given and received. However, when this center is blocked or out of balance, giving and/or receiving love is restricted.

The fifth chakra is the Throat Center, the Thyroid gland, and "seat of the Will," according to Cayce. Its color is blue; planet, Uranus. It is associated with the Cervical plexus $(C_1$-

C_4). Imbalances in metabolism are often a result of thyroid problems.

The sixth chakra, according to Cayce, is the Crown Chakra, associated with the Pineal gland. Its color is indigo; planet, Mercury. It is the center for soul-memory and imagination.

The seventh chakra is the Third Eye Center and located in the middle of the forehead. It is associated with the Pituitary gland. Its color is violet (the mixing of purple with white); planet is Jupiter. It is the master gland of the body, highest connecting point with the Spirit.[8]

Now having gained a larger perspective of the anatomy of the body, let's look again at the "major incoordination traced to the 9th dorsal area" for the man (2387) in the sanitarium (See *Down the Spine* section in the chapter on Cayce's four patterns of spinal massage). Relating this to plexuses and chakras and using contemporary language, another level of meaning becomes available. The 9th dorsal or solar plexus refers to the abdominal area – that place where much of our digestion and elimination takes place. It's associated psychologically with our thinking center, our ambition, our ego. This is where one has a "gut feeling," is "weak bellied" or "can't stomach" something. Just as food passes down the throat into the stomach to be digested, so do our thoughts, beliefs, ideas, and self-worth move up and down the spinal cord and affect the sympathetic nervous system. If congestion occurs around the 9th dorsal, it's obvious that the person may be having difficulty digesting not only his food but also his self-image or self-worth. In fact, letters from 2387's sister described just such a situation. He needed to become "absorbed in an interest," she wrote. Clearly depressed, the man's thoughts, ambition, and ego weren't strong enough to create a healthy balance between body, mind, and spirit. Taking into consideration his medical diagnosis of "involutional depression," Cayce's description of a physical and mental breakdown with an incoordination in the 9th dorsal area (T_9), and letters from 2387's sister describing his behavior, a block or congestion is revealed in the third chakra. He first lost control of his emotions, and then they turned inward. It's possible that he was greatly frustrated in his personal relationships or work. Unable to resolve his problems, they turned inward, made him sick, and thereby forced others to take care of him – a typical pattern for the third chakra. The reading stated that the incoordination was due to a loss of "vital energy."

Thus we see that a comprehensive knowledge of spinal massage and its relationship to plexuses and chakras greatly enhances our ability to help someone become better coordinated in body, mind and spirit. A spinal rub then becomes not only a form of physical therapy, but a profoundly compassionate expression in the hands of a loving and caring person.

If the massage therapist chooses to use short leg technique and spinal massage as part of the treatment, I believe there is a much greater chance for the client to gain a deeper understanding of his situation and reach a state of balance and coordination physically, mentally, and spiritually. For spinal massage as described in this book is based on a massage along the spine that directs its attention to the sympathetic ganglia lying just in front of the transverse processes of the vertebrae. The Cayce readings, osteopathic massage, neuropathic massage, and massage by any massage therapist with some knowledge of anatomy and physiology all support the beneficial effect of spinal massage on the sympathetic nervous system, and consequently the whole person.

In answer to a question about the value of osteopathic treatments, Edgar Cayce included a statement about the sympathetic ganglia that certainly would apply to the practice of massage. "Stimulating ganglia from which impulses arise – either sympathetically or functionally – must then be helpful in the body gaining an equilibrium" (E.C., 902-1). Equilibrium is what each of us is continually seeking. What better way to help another pass through doors which open this possibility.

Endnotes:

[1] This is not the only possibility with a short leg. An osteopath, for example, might discover lesions on the spine.

However, the youngster had been examined by a medical doctor and nothing pathological was diagnosed.

[2] See the following:

a) John Sarno, M.D., *Mind Over Back Pain* (New York: Berkeley Books, 1982).

b) Morgan Sargent, "Psychosomatic Backache," *The New England Journal of Medicine*, Vol. 234, No. 13, (March 28, 1946,) pp. 427-430.

c) Thomas H. Holmes, M.D. and Harold G. Wolff, M.D., "Life Situations, Emotions, and Backache," *Psychosomatic Medicine*, Vol. 14 (Jan-Feb No. 1, 1952), pp. 18-33.

[3] A short leg and resulting musculoskeletal imbalance in no way contradicts the findings in athletes where there is a tendency for hamstring pulls in those who have a greater strength ratio between quadriceps and hamstrings. See Wm. Southmayd, M.D. and Marshall Hoffman, *Sports Health*, "Hamstring Strains (Hamstring Pulls)," (New York: Putnam Publishing Co., 1981) pp. 239-242.

[4] See Dr. John Sarno's *Mind Over Back Pain* for an interesting book on the relationship between chronic back pain, the autonomic nervous system, and the mind. The Edgar Cayce Readings are also an invaluable resource for insights into mind-body relationships.

[5] The short leg technique may reveal a primary pattern (e.g. the pelvis) before the complaint in the area (such as the neck) can be treated.

[6] See Irvin Korr, D.O. "Proprioceptors and Somatic Dysfunction," *The Collected Papers of Irvin M. Korr*, (Colorado Springs, CO: American Academy of Osteopathy, 1979) pp. 200-207.

[7] Dychtwald, Ken, Ph.D. *Bodymind*. (Los Angeles: Jeremy P Tarcher, Inc. 1950) p. 163.

[8] For a more complete explanation of these chakras, see Edgar Cayce's readings on the Revelation.

Chapter Six

WARS AND WARRIORS OF THE BODY

When things have gone wrong in a person's life, so that his personality is deeply disturbed, this shows itself first in nervous troubles, for it is our nervous system which is the most fragile.
— Paul Tormier, *The Healing of Persons*

Middle age, the time of the popularized "mid-life crisis" is often a difficult period for many of us. I can recall a reading by Edgar Cayce in which a person in their late forties was advised to alter dietary habits because the body's needs at that age were changing due to its metabolic processes beginning to differ from when younger. Changes in amounts of food, kind of food, and exercise were some of the recommendations. What particularly attracted me was the awareness that the body responds differently in middle age, and that many of the symptoms described in this reading, as well as many others for middle-aged people, are very similar: loss of vitality, constipation, bad breath, difficulty in moving one's joints, and poor digestion.

In a reading for a 50-year-old man, let's call him "Tom," Cayce approached Tom's concerns in a fascinating way. Tom particularly wanted to know why he had an itching, burning sensation all over his body that caused him to want to rub himself right down to the bone. He was also experiencing constipation and times of bad breath, tingling in his arms and legs, and a general lack of vitality. He may even have worried about having cancer, for the reading mentions that there was no malignancy — just irritating symptoms and a great deal of *worry* about middle-age.

Tom's prognosis was very good. Though the reading acknowledged that his physical problems had been there for a long time, they were treatable and he could look forward to living many more years with opportunity for his mental, and spiritual growth.

The cause of his problem went back many years to an

injury to his right side below the liver. Now take a look at the domino effect this set in motion. Initially, adhesions built up at the site of the injury. Lesions formed in the lacteal ducts and the gall duct, areas having a lot to do with digestion and assimilations, especially the absorption of fats into the body. Poor assimilations led to poor digestion and regurgitation. Over time a "superacidity" was created in the body affecting organs and eliminations. This toxicity in the organs eventually affected the blood, especially the hepatic circulation (between the kidneys and the liver). Circulation slowed down in the superficial and arterial flow of blood as well as the return or venous flow. This was the cause of the "crawling or creeping" sensation under the skin and even down to the bone.

Toxic forces in the blood prevented adequate growth of leucocytes (white blood cells), these are the "warriors" in the blood supply, designed to fight off infections and to carry away natural waste matter from cellular metabolism. For example, whenever some kind of strep was present in his system, the warriors couldn't carry it away. Consequently, there would be periods when Tom had bad breath, burning feelings in his stomach, tingling in his limbs, and lack of energy.

When the toxins affected his nervous system, he broke out in a cold sweat, or felt cold and clammy and shook all over. The reading said:

This is a reaction to not only the sympathetic or vegetative nerve system (which is the double system that runs along the cerebrospinal and functions for the coordinating or the governing between the mental body and the physical body), but to the cerebrospinal system (which is rather the deeper nerve forces that supply energies to the various portions of the body, the organs and the locomotory centers, for responses). (E. C., 1055-1)

Sometimes Tom would get depressed because of memory lapse. Cayce's response is another interesting example of how mind and body affect one another.

These were not mental aberrations; they were the effect of the two nerve systems, as it were, warring one with another owing to the poisons that have been allowed to accumulate through ... improper assimilation. (Edgar Cayce, 1055-1)

Recommendations for treatment began by making it clear that much of the responsibility for full recovery was in Tom's hands. He would have to be patient and persistent in following suggestions. Moreover, he must have faith – a faith that believed in both following the treatments and believing they would work. Then he could expect a longer life greatly improved with "opportunities and activities" for his body, mind, and spirit.

Specific suggestions for treatment included castor oil packs to help loosen the adhesions below the liver, a compound taken internally to help with assimilation, colonics to help eliminations, and a massage of the cerebrospinal nervous system with a mixture of oils stimulating in their effect.

Massage in the whole of the cerebrospinal system, from the base of the head to the end of the spine; and then not so much[1] along the sciatic nerves along the lower limbs, and then across the abdominal area – but not the lower portions; rather from the diaphragm area and about same. (E.C., 1055-1)

The massage of the cerebrospinal nervous system is what particularly interests us, although we must always keep in mind that massage is only one of the treatment suggestions offered and that its effect is related to the application of the entire program for treatment. Earlier in the reading, the cerebrospinal nervous system is defined as the nervous system that is "the deeper nerve forces that supply energies to the various portions of the body, the organs and the locomotory centers, for responses" (E.C., 1055-1).

So the cerebrospinal nervous system is the brain, the spinal cord, and, I believe, the branches or rami of the spinal nerves as they leave the vertebrae (see illustrations 1,2,3, & 8). This is an important concept for massage because massage of the cerebrospinal nervous system is a little different from the sympathetic system; massage along sensory nerve pathways is another distinction.

To understand this, let's look at the spinal column (see illustration 5). It is a flexible column supporting the head and protecting the spinal cord. The spine is made up of a series of bones called vertebrae: 7 cervical, 12 thoracic (or dorsal), 5 lumbar, 5 sacral fused into the sacrum, and 4 coccygeal fused into the coccyx.

All the vertebrae look pretty much alike (see illustration 2). Except for the first cervical vertebra, they all have a flat, rounded body with a spinous process projecting backward and downward. All but the sacrum and coccyx have a central opening, the vertebral foramen, which houses the spinal cord. Each vertebra has two transverse processes projecting laterally. Leading from each vertebral foramen to the outside on each side are smaller openings called intervertebral foramen. These openings provide an opening for spinal nerves which branch off from the spinal cord and go to different organs, muscles, and glands of the body (see illustration 8 and 6, respectively).

Thirty-one pairs of spinal nerves emerge from the spinal cord (see illustration 3). Just after a spinal nerve emerges from the vertebral column it divides into several branches called rami. There is an anterior, posterior, and a white ramus. The anterior and posterior rami supply nerves to skeletal muscles and skin. The white rami contains nerve fibers of the sympathetic nervous system.

What is interesting here is the Cayce readings' description of the cerebrospinal nervous system (or the central nervous system[2]) as supplying energies and nerve impulses not only throughout the body and for its movement (locomotion), but to organs which are usually considered part of the peripheral nervous system, the sympathetic nervous system. Therefore, I would conclude that in Cayce's readings, the cerebrospinal nervous system includes not only the brain and spinal cord, but also the branches or rami of the spinal nerves emerging from the spinal column: the posterior, anterior, and white rami.

128

With this understanding, his directions for "massage in the whole of the cerebrospinal system" starts to make some sense, for there are going to be many other readings where the emphasis of the massage either shifts to the sympathetic nervous system or to both cerebrospinal and sympathetic nervous systems (see illustration 7). In the reading for Tom, the massage is directly on the *whole* cerebrospinal nervous system from the base of the head to the end of the spine, and then down the limbs following the sciatic nerve (see endnote 1).

Location and direction of the massage are important. In Tom, remember, the two nervous systems are frequently warring with each other and circulation to the limbs and back is slow. So massage of the entire central nervous system, including all branches of the spinal nerves as they leave the spinal column from the head down, stimulates the outward and downward flow of nerve impulses (see illustration 9). This would, in effect, stimulate movement of blood away from the heart or through the arteries. It would include stimulation to nerve impulses along nerve pathways to muscles, and into into the branches leading to the sympathetic ganglia, to the major nerve (sciatic) going down the legs, and to major locomotory centers in the low back and pelvis – the lumbar and sacral plexuses.[3]

While the massage and oils were stimulating in a direction from the brain down and out through the spinal cord to various "portions of the body, the organs and the locomotory centers," other treatments were affecting elimination and digestion in a general movement to remove toxins from the body.

Unfortunately, Tom's condition didn't improve much over the next 18 months in spite of four readings and being in the care of a physician. According to the readings, the major reason for lack of improvement was his inability to follow the suggestions completely, especially regarding his diet and attitude. In his last reading, Tom is told: "There is not a great deal of change" even though there are times when he feels better and other times when he feels discouraged. "Most of this as we find is a matter of attitude of mind of the body."

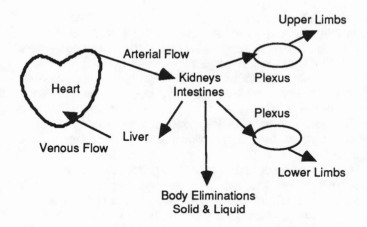

Because the "disturbing factors" were so "deep-seated," he had been warned over and over to be patient and persistent. Yet, Tom remained discouraged and depressed.

Why didn't Tom get better? There isn't enough information in follow-up material to know more, but there is the fascinating metaphor of war throughout the reading. Tom's cerebrospinal and sympathatic nervous system were warring, and some organs were warring with the elimination systems. Perhaps Tom was being told to be more of a warrior himself – to persist, to go on resolutely and stubbornly in spite of opposition, to have faith that his forces would win, continue to exist, and create opportunties for a better and longer life.

The warrior forces exist in all of us, but in times of crisis we need to strengthen and encourage them – to call on them. For the leucocytes are the warriors which help our immune system fight off poisons, bacteria, and viruses. When we become discouraged and depressed, our immune system reflects these feelings and emotions, and we become ill. We need to acquire some of the valuable traits of warriors. As our mind adopts these traits, the very atoms of our body adopt them, each taking up the battle against

130

illness. "In every physical being, the whole body is made up of the atomic forces of the system, *with the mind of each atom*, as it is builded, *supervised by the whole mental mind of the body*.... (E.C., 137-81, my italics)."

A wonderful vision into this warrior mentality is also presented in Dr. A.T. Still's autobiography.

...there is much evidence that mind is imparted to the corpuscles of the blood before it does its work.

Every corpuscle goes like a man in the army, with full instructions where to go, and with unerring precision it does its work – whether it be in the formation of a hair or throwing of a spot of delicate tinting at certain distances on a peacock's back.

God does not find it necessary to make one of these spots of beauty at a time; He simply endows the corpuscles with mind, and in obediance to His law each one of these soldiers of life goes like a man in the army, with full instructions as to the duty he is to perform.[4]

As therapists, we need to be sensitive to our clients, for at times we must convey to them the need to become as warriors and to be aware of the warrior's place in their recovery. At other times, we must convey an aura of love, relaxation and gentleness, creating an environment of peace, unconditional love and support.

We must use our skilled judgment and experience to discern the right approach for our clients. We know from the readings that obtaining a history of bodily injury and traumas from the client is paramount. And since we don't have an Edgar Cayce to consult, we must listen to our patients carefully, relying on our intuition for guidance. Then, as we massage the body, we learn to "hear" the body's messages – our hands becoming like sensors, discovering the subtle tightnesses, displacements, blockages and incoordinations. In this way, we can respond to the specific needs of each individual, and healing can occur. However, as we learned from Tom's example, we can only facilitate healing; true healing comes from *within* the client. It is his or her will, attitude and faith that makes the body ripe for revitalization and healing.

Endnotes:

[1] The phrase "not so much" should probably be read parenthetically to indicate less amount of time spent massaging along the sciatic nerve and down the leg.

[2] "We find in the activities of the organs themselves that the brain forces are very good. Reflexes are not at all times good, owing to the inability of coordinating the cerebrospinal or the central [nervous system] and the sympathetic nerve forces of the body." (Edgar Cayce Reading 2491-1, p.2)

[3] Plexus is a braid-like network of nerves; more on this in the chapter on plexuses.

[4] Andrew T. Still, D.O., *Autobiography of A.t. Still* (Kirksville, MO: Published by the Author, 1897) pp. 223-224.

Chapter Seven

THE POWER OF COORDINATION

"It is a very hard problem to have a home and a career and both be a success" (E.C., 1125-3). Cayce was speaking on that September day, 1941, to a 61-year-old female osteopath, conveying how well she understood the difficulty of trying to be in two places at the same time and now was fully gaining the "awakening or realization" of having a "home and a career." This could easily be a statement in any number of current newspapers, magazines, or books describing the situation facing many working women today. We tend to think this is only a recent problem, but the women's movement goes back to the nineteenth century and earlier. Working women have always had to face the pull between the home and the work place.

In a letter (9/23/41) to Edgar Cayce requesting advice and help, this woman described the difficulties she was having at home. Her husband, twenty years younger, was less educated, made considerably less money than she, drank, had "a bad case of inferiority complex," had had a nervous breakdown and had spent some time at a Veteran's Hospital. He continually belittled her and picked on their son. She had tried unsuccessfully to get him to move out.

Four years later, she told Cayce she never separated from him because "I thought he needed me but now I think I have made a bad mistake. I should have separated long ago and he would have been better off." Her son was now 18 years old and going to Swarthmore College. "I have my practice here and would like to see my son through college. What shall I do?" She also wanted mental and spiritual peace for herself.

In contemporary language, here is a woman under considerable stress: long hours working as an osteopath, a difficult marriage, worry about paying her son's college tuition, concerns about her son's health and her own – physically, mentally, and spiritually. The advice given in the reading was to try to come to an understanding and agreement with her husband. They should try to help each other, not by shouting or arguing, but by finding what was best for the other. If a divorce was the best solution, then agreements could be reached in the spirit of assisting the other. The financial responsibility for the son also had to be considered.

This stressful condition had been going on for years. Four years earlier she had requested a health reading. She sent Cayce the following information. "I have had sinus trouble. I am too heavy and whenever I try to reduce, I get too tired. I tried to reduce since Christmas and got a heavy cold. Do I have T.B.? How can I help constipation?"

What is extremely interesting is how the reading handles her complaints. The reading is divided into three parts, but not the customary division found in most health readings. Usually, there is a very brief statement of cause followed by diagnoses of the blood, the nerve system, and the organs. Then a specific course of treatment is outlined. But in this reading, the first third is devoted to a description of how the body functions in relationship to "the whole of the conditions and environs under which the body labors from a mental and material angle, as well as the spiritual" (E.C., 1125-1). It is the second third which traces the condition of her physical body followed by specific suggestions for treatment.

It is not surprising that the recommended therapies encompass a range of activities designed to follow "the rule or law of the profession of the body." Cayce, in effect, is saying "take a look at your own field of medicine for self-guidance." For one of the principle tenets of osteopathy is to treat the body as a whole (unit) in order to "bring about those conditions where the body-physical, the body-mental, yea the body spiritual may coordinate, and cooperate, in keeping the producing of health rather than disease in the physical body" (E.C., 1125-2).

The reading is making clear to the doctor that given her particular education as an osteopath, she should understand that treatment of pathological conditions alone is fruitless, for unless "...the causes or the attitudes of the body mentally, and without a better *coordination* of the ideals of the body in its *relationships* to material, to mental, as arise from its spiritual concept, are made to be in better *coordination*, there can not be any real help" (E.C., 1125-1, my italics). In other words, if treatment only consists of a *physical* diagnosis and treatment plan, there is the very high probability that the symptoms will appear in another part of the body unless the whole of the person's relationship with other persons, environment, and spiritual endeavors are considered. Cayce's recommendations included attitudinal adjustments, first; mechanical adjustments, second; followed by vibrations set up by the radio-active appliance, meditation, use of Atomidine,[1] exercises, and dietary recommendations to keep an acid/alkaline balance.

Let's look then at her relationship with others in the home and work environment. According to her letter of Sept. 23, 1941, and the date of a physical reading for her then 13-year-old son, February 1, 1937, the situation and relationships at home were deteriorating. Her husband had been hospitalized because of a nervous breakdown. Her son seemed physically weak; he would come down with colds easily, run a subnormal temperature, and have chronic abdominal pain. Naturally, the mother suspected appendicitis and feared he might also have T.B. (His reading revealed an anemic condition and poor digestion due to a reaction from or side effect of previous innoculations.)

Dealing with these situations alone would have been overwhelming. But in addition, she was seeing patients daily, giving physical help to some and mental or emotional hope to others – the purpose which guided her to "the very *choice* of the entity as to a professional!"

Acknowledging the difficulty in her home life, the reading counseled her to show the same attitude and concern she gave her patients to her husband and son: "Then why not take this policy, take this attitude, *in all the relationships* of the entity's experience?" (E.C., 1125-1, my italics). She had very much considered *herself* the victim: "There are then attitudes – not assumed but as are ofttimes considered by the body *as being thrust upon* the body, by its correlations with individuals and its activities" (E.C., 1125-1, my italics). Instead of looking at circumstances in this light – resenting, hating, or being disagreeable in the home environment and relationships – she was advised to "*coordinate*" her spiritual ideals with same and replace her animosity with patience and understanding. Without this change, her physical symptoms could not go away, for one part of her being would not be in accord with that part which seeks "mental and spiritual rest"; that part which believes in an eternal, spiritual, creative being; that part which needs to accept the concept of healing as the coordination not only of the body within, but of all of the body's relationships in all situations and in all of its environments.

It's gratifying to report that this woman followed the advice given to her. Although we don't know how the relationship with her husband was eventually resolved, she was still practicing osteopathy when she was 75 and lived well into her 80s. Her son graduated from Swarthmore and entered the service as an engineer, married, and had at least one child.

The concept of coordination is fundamental to an understanding of how and why certain suggestions for treatments are given in the Cayce readings. In an extensive series of readings given to a 38-year-old homemaker, this concept is clearly presented. Again, we see the body-mind relationship explored. Having achieved a state of good physical health, in the following reading she is advised to pay more attention to her "mental and material attitude" and, "...to conditions without as well as within. For the whole of the experience of an individual entity in a material plane is the coordinating and cooperation of Creative Forces from without to the divine within, as to keeping an activity that may bring into manifestations health and happiness" (E.C., 1158-8). The theme is clear: coordination is achieved as an individual uses his or her resources in a cooperative manner with larger Creative Forces.

Many of the 38 readings she received over an eight-year span covered a gamut of minor health problems. However, in the eleventh reading (E.C., 1158-11), an unusual response is given to what appears to be a simple question. "Would Squibb's Dicalcium Phosphate with viosterol be wise for me to take?" The reply suggested,

...this would depend very much upon how often the mechanical adjustments osteopathically are made, and the massage given. For as understood by the body, and by the one that would make the mechanical or ostepathic adjustments, or the massage or masseuse activity, there is every force in the body to recreate its own self – if the various portions of the system are coordinating and cooperating one with another. (E.C., 1158-11)

Then follows a crucial statement of the use of osteopathy as a treatment:

Hence the reason why, as we have so oft given from the sources here, that mechanical adjustments as may be administered by a thorough or serious osteopathic manipulator may nearer adjust the system for its perfect unison of activity than most any other means – save under acute or specific conditions; and even then the more oft such become necessary. (E.C., 1158-11)

From this, I understand Cayce's source to be saying that even though many other types of treatments are recommended, they tend to be more specific in their reaction within the body. For example, the use of "Abbets Dulcet Bar, Dicalcium Phosphate will help the body to become less acid, and help with cold or congestion or shivering feelings." But specific osteopathic adjustments "are to release activities in such a way and manner that the endocrine glands, the absorption through the activities of the lacteals, will PRODUCE these elements in greater quantity for the system" (E.C., 1158-11). The idea was not to allow the body to become dependent on the prescription, but to let the body produce its own elements for helping with absorption and maintain the acid/alkaline balance. The activity of the endocrine glands – specifically to aid the lacteals and the "nerve plexus just below the gall duct" – has to be stimulated to increase its activity in order for the body to function in a more coordinated manner.

The massage "is for the superficial circulation, to keep attunement as it were between the superficial circulation or the lymph and the exterior portion with the activities of the body" (E.C., 1158-11). Again there is stated a crucial concept – this time specifically about the massage. In her first reading, symptoms are described in relation to the blood supply. There is a tendency for anemia characterized by fewer red blood cells, tiredness, aching and feeling of heaviness in the torso or the shoulders, headaches, burning sensation in the throat or eyes, and dryness. This is caused by poor lymph circulation and "the incoordination between the deeper circulation and the superficial."

It is important to recognize a deeper understanding behind the diagnosis and treatment suggestions. All had to be followed in the order suggested. Massage was one mode of therapy, and in this particular reading its purpose is clearly stated not only for ll58, but in general, regarding its ability to help processes of coordination.

In any case, the incoordination between the deep and superficial circulation involves a cleansing process of the lacteals and "the activative forces between the superficial and the deeper circulation" (E.C., 1158-1). This is to be done by using castor oil packs and "gentle massage." The castor oil stimulates the liver function of producing bile and absorption through the lacteals which are in the duodenum.[2]

The massage stimulates the flow of blood precisely at those points where the superficial and deeper circulation meet. Remember, as blood leaves the heart, it travels through arteries, then to arterioles, and into the capillary system. From here it flows into the venous system for its return to the heart and to the lungs for reoxygenation. So the capillary system is where it's at. This is the transference point – or where the superficial and deep circulation coordinate with each other. When they don't coordinate, oxygen deficiency is created in the blood, waste products fail to get eliminated, muscles gradually get sore, headaches occur, and other symptoms of toxicity can appear. Increased activity only makes matters worse. Eliminations slow down; digestion is out of balance, causing acidity and feelings of heaviness. The heart and lungs slow down and are unable to provide the needed oxygen and nutrients to parts of the body, and so on.

So the gentle use of massage is very effective to help stimulate the flow of blood through the capillaries and through the muscles in its return to the heart. It activates a cleansing process that helps coordinate the circulation of both blood and lymph.

In so many physical readings, the information frequently given strives to coordinate one part of the body with another – for example, the coordination of nerve ganglia with muscles, or a plexus with circulation, and so on. But in the readings reviewed in this chapter (and in so many other readings) coordination is placed in a larger context, one in which the body exists as a physical, mental, and spiritual being in an environment of relationships with other human beings – all within a larger cosmos with a Divine and Creative Force.

I believe this is the heart of most all of the physical readings. Coordination is a state of balance and harmony, and according to Webster's Dictionary, an arrangement "so as to act together in a smooth, concerted way." This is the essence of health, and a primary concern for any therapist.

Endnotes:

1 Atomidine is an atomic form of iodine often recommended in the readings for internal use to help balance glandular activity, always in extremely *small* doses. However, its use can be dangerous. Therefore, I suggest you do not use or recommend this until you have a full understanding of the manner and proportions Cayce gave. Of course, any time internal use is recommended I believe you should not proceed to ingest the item until you are sure you understand its purpose, effect and the manner and proportion by which it is to be used. Even then, your particular body or the combination with other medicines you may be using might cause a reaction quite different from that described. So be

careful and fully informed.

[2] See William A. McGarey, M.D. *Physicians Reference Notebook.* Virginia Beach, VA: A.R.E. Press, 1983.

Chapter Eight

HYDROTHERAPY, OILS & FORMULAS

Water has been used in healing throughout time. Water is Spirit, water is Life, and an important part of a holistic health regimen. Water helps the body restore energy flow, remove waste products and toxins, normalize circulation, increase the effectiveness of the immune system in preventing disease, relieve pain, and maintain health.

The Edgar Cayce readings frequently prescribed water in its various forms — liquid, solid (ice) and gas (vapor/steam) — to aid in the healing process. Examples include: whirlpools, steam/fume baths, sitz baths, epsom salts baths, tub baths, and colonic irrigations.

CAYCE HYDROTHERAPIES

COLONIC IRRIGATION
In a letter to 3280-1, Mr. Cayce explained:

...hydrotherapy, practically in everyone, includes (unless it is made specific that it is not to be used) colonic irrigation. This I think, under the hands of a good hydrotherapist, is one of the best ways of preventing a prolapsus, but I am sure your doctor should be able to advise you respecting this. (E.C., 3280-1, p.10)

What is a colonic? It is a cleansing procedure of the colon or large intestine, which is about four to five feet in length. A professional machine is used to gradually fill the colon with a gentle water pressure and then alternately empty out waste matter using a mild siphon effect. Thus, the diverticula or pockets of the colon are cleansed, and peristalsis, the muscular contractions by which the colon propels waste matter along, is stimulated. This helps to improve eliminations. In contrast, an enema is given to relieve constipation and generally reaches only the descending colon on the left side of the body.

The readings recommend adding salt, baking soda and Glyco-Thymoline,[1] an alkaline antiseptic, to the water in order to prevent irritation and inflammation. The amounts vary with each individual, but an average is one heaping teaspoon sea salt and one level teaspoon baking soda added to the first quart of water, and one tablespoon of Glyco-Thymoline added to the last two quarts of water.

... then have a high enema. This means a colonic enema, *not* just a movement of the lower portion of the colon but *throughout* the colon area; that there may be a setting up of a coordination in the eliminating system. (E.C., 1055-1)

When eliminations become sluggish, waste matter accumulates and affects other organs, causing dis-ease, as well as disease. The hydrotherapies, colonics, massage, diet changes, lifestyle changes, and osteopathy all help the body return to balance and health.

Some disturbances are indicated in the digestive forces of the body. These are from lack of proper eliminations even though there are regularities – the eliminations need to be increased from these angles. This may be done in no better manner than by having colonic irrigations occasionally and by including in the diet such things as figs, rhubarb and the like. (E.C., 4003-1)

In reading 5609-1, Cayce told a 41-year-old man that colonics would not only help his spinal adjustments to hold better, but that his whole digestive system would be aided.

...but occasionally have those of the *colonic* irrigations to relieve the pressure in the colon region, so that – as the corrections are made in the cerebro-spinal system – these may *remain* in their correct order. We will also by same remove that mucus and that tendency for discharge in the rectum itself, and in those portions from which the body finds those inflammations arising. We will find also that the digestion will be improved. While the body eats a plenty in the present, yet in the *assimilating* of that *taken* does not *always* follow that those taken feel or agree just well *with* the

142

body. This we find will be improved by this removing of these pressures in the intestinal tract. This will also tend to make a better coordinating activity with the liver itself, *provided* there is not *too* much of this used – once a month for two to three months (that is, two to three irrigations), then *rest* for the period before they are taken again, see? And have *this* done by one who understands, and not [one who] just bungles along with it! (E.C., 5609-1)

STEAM/FUME BATHS

The steams/fumes were recommended to increase eliminations through the skin and lungs. A fume means that a substance added to boiling water in the steam cabinet vaporizes; it then settles on the skin and is absorbed through the pores. Some of the more frequently mentioned additives were atomidine, witch hazel, pine needle oil and wintergreen oil.

A steam cabinet with an opening at the top for the head to remain outside is preferable to a steam room, although Cayce did, on occassion, recommend a full steam room. (See reading 3564-1 in the chapter on Swedish massage) The steam cabinet procedure does allow for the pulse to be monitored and cold cloths to be applied at the base of the neck and forehead to prevent headaches and light-headedness. Drinking water before having a steam is recommended. After fifteen or twenty minutes in the cabinet, a tepid shower is taken to wash off the impurities that have been brought to the surface of the skin. Having a steam before a massage is relaxing and aids in absorption of the massage oils.

EPSOM SALTS BATHS

An Epsom Salts bath is another way to induce perspiration and increase eliminations. It was recommended for circulation, rheumatism, sciatica, injuries, incoordination, arthritis, muscle pain and soreness. Because an Epsom Salts bath can be very stimulating and increase the circulation and heart rate, it should not be taken by people with high blood pressure or heart conditions.

The amount of Epsom Ealts varied with each person, but an average is five pounds to a 20 gallon tub. (Very large amounts were given for arthritis; it is advisable to follow the readings on this.) After soaking 10 to 20 minutes in 102° to 106° tub, one wraps up in a towel and continues sweating for 30 minutes before showering off and having a massage.

SITZ BATHS

Though its benefits are too often overlooked or ignored, a Sitz bath is a very effective form of hydrotherapy. By alternating the water temperature, circulation is affected to the organs and glands of the lower abdomen and pelvic area, decreasing congestion, inflammation and discomfort. Specifically, it is known to help relieve hemorrhoids and constipation, as well as bladder, prostate and uterine problems.

Two tubs are used that look like large easy chairs. They are designed to keep only the hips and pelvic area in the water while the feet remain on the floor. One tub contains warm water, 100° to 106°, and the other contains cold water, 60° to 65°. Beginning with warm water, one alternates sitting three times for two to four minutes, ending with the cold tub.

WHIRLPOOLS/HOT TUBS

Whirlpools and hot tubs are very effective in relieving muscular discomfort and pain from injuries, increasing circulation, reducing inflammation and arthritis pain, and removing embedded dirt and dead skin cells. There seems to be an added healing force in moving water which relaxes as well as energizes the body.

The therapeutic effect of all baths is dependent upon the temperature and length of time in the water. Hot water is sedating, relaxing and soothing but can deplete the physical of minerals if overdone. Care should be taken not to stay in more than 10 to 15 minutes. Cold water is stimulating, restorative and helps build resistance to disease. Most of us would rather take warm baths, but if we only realized how valuable colder water is, we would change our bathing habits.

CAYCE MASSAGE OILS AND LINAMENTS

Oils were more than simply a lubricant for massage strokes in Cayce's eyes. His most commonly recommended massage oils were olive oil, peanut oil, Nujol (also known as Usoline, Russian white oil or mineral oil), cocoa butter and castor oil. There are many other massage oils on the market, such as almond, sesame, avocado, sunflower, safflower, apricot kernal, etc., but they were not mentioned by Cayce. Many massage therapists who are unaware of the therapeutic effects of Cayce's oils use powder, lotions which dry out quickly, or other more expensive concoctions.

OLIVE OIL

Olive oil is food for muscles and mucous membranes, according to the Cayce readings, and was suggested for use both internally and externally. Many combinations include sassafras, pine needle oil, tincture of benzoin, cedarwood oil or wintergreen to be added to olive oil.

An ancient formula calls for equal parts of olive oil and myrrh. The olive oil is usually warmed first and then the myrrh is added, otherwise they do not mix together. This formula was recommended for massage in the following reading:

Q-7. How often should the manipulations or massage be given?
A-7. Three times each week.
Q-8. How often should the *olive oil and tincture of myrrh* be applied?
A-8. As indicated, the massage of these properties into the spine should be applied particularly soon after the use of the deep therapy machine. For, while there is the activity of the electrical forces in the body, the ganglia along the spine will respond to the necessary forces for absorption better than when there is less electrical force in the body, see? Hence, these massages would be given in this manner, for the activity of such would be as this:

The oil, as it were, is to relax the tendencies for contraction through impulses that are lacking, as indicated, or that are excessive (for both occur), in the ganglia of the cerebrospinal system.

The myrrh, as an activative force with the oil, acts as a healing influence to the tendency of inflammation or *drying* of the texture or tendril effect of muscular activities of the system. (E.C., 372-8)

The combination of olive oil and myrrh was advised for scar tissue in reading 440-3.

For, the therapeutic value of the properties given to the skin itself is as follows: As given, as known and held by the ancients more than the present modes of medication, olive oil – properly prepared (hence pure olive oil should always be used) – is one of the most effective agents for stimulating muscular activity, or mucous-membrane activity, that may be applied to a body. Olive oil, then, combined with the Tincture of Myrrh will be very effective; for the Tincture of Myrrh acts with the pores of the skin in such a manner as to strike in, causing the circulation to be carried to affected parts where tissue has been in the nature of folds – or scar tissue, produced from superficial activity from the active forces in the body itself, in making for coagulation in any portion of the system, whether external or internal. (E.C., 440-3)

Another scar massage formula was given in reading 2015-10: camphorated oil (olive oil and camphor), lanolin and peanut oil. This individual was to receive a daily massage over many months with "patience, persistence and faith" if the removal of scars was to be fully realized.

PEANUT OIL
Peanut oil is suggested for use alone or in combination with other oils for low vitality, fatigue, arthritis, poor circulation and paralysis:

Daily, for at least half to an hour and a half, massage the body; not rudely, not crudely, not with the attempt to make adjustments – for many weeks yet. Massage with Peanut oil, – yes, the lowly Peanut oil has in its combination that which will aid in creating in the superficial circulation, and in the superficial structural forces, as well as in the skin and blood, those influences that make more pliable the skin, muscles, nerves and tendons, that go to make up the assistance to structural portions of the body. Its absorption and its radiation through the body will also strengthn the activities of the structural body itself. (E.C., 2968-1)

Although Cayce said peanut oil does not turn rancid on the body, any oil can go rancid very quickly Therefore, all stock bottles of massage oils should be kept refrigerated and old bottles replaced with fresh ones. Of course, refrigerated oils must be brought up to body temperature before using them in a massage.

Peanut oil was the most frequently mentioned oil in the Cayce readings, particularly for arthritis (which he said was preventable through its use), and massage along the spine. In reading 1206-13, he said if peanut rubs were given once a week, one would never develop rheumatism.

NUJOL

Nujol, also called Russian White Oil, Usoline or mineral oil, is found in prescribed formulas for paralysis, injured ligaments, leg and foot pain, muscular sprain, strains and backache.

Q-4. Please give me something that will ease my back.
A-4. This is a very good specific:
To 1 ounce of Olive Oil, add:
     Russian White Oil, 2 ounces,
     Witch hazel, 1/2 ounce,
     Tincture of Benzoin, 1/2 ounce,
     Oil of Sassafras, 20 minims,
     Coal Oil, 6 ounces.
It'll be necessary to shake this together, for it will tend to separate; but a small quantity massaged in the cerebrospinal system or over sprains, joints, swellings, bruises, will take out the inflammation or pain. (E.C., 326-5) [Gladys Davis Turner's note indicates that the same rub was suggested in 243-18 which followed the reading above.]

COCOA BUTTER

Cocoa butter is advised instead of oils for massage of infants and children, as well as for spinal massage of the cerebrospinal nervous system in adults.

Each evening, then, when preparing the body for bed, we would massage the spine – gently, not deeply but gently – with all the Glyco-Thymoline the body will absorb.

Each morning, just after the bath, massage with Cocoa Butter; ALWAYS AWAY FROM THE HEAD, in a gentle circular motion, on either side of the spine; from the base of the brain DOWNWARD to the 9th dorsal, and then from the end of the spine UPWARD to the 9th dorsal, see? (E.C., 2999-1)

Each evening, then, we would apply this: Take a small quantity of cocoa butter – an ounce of same. To this we would add Oil of Cedar 10 minims, Oil of Sassafras 5 minims. Massage this thoroughly together, see, or mix or stir. Then use a small quantity to massage the whole cerebro-spinal system, especially over the area of the 8th and 9th dorsal, and the sacral and lumbar area – see? (E.C., 357-1)

CASTOR OIL

Castor Oil is a very stable oil which does not turn rancid easily. It is not used for a general massage because it is too thick to rub over large areas. However, equal parts of castor oil, olive oil and peanut oil make an excellent mixture for general massage. Castor oil alone, used with an infra-red heat lamp for 15-20 minutes, can be used on a local specific area for muscular or joint pain, arthritis and rheumatism.

In the Middle Ages, castor oil was known as "Palma Christi" or "Palm of Christ" because it was so helpful and healing. Cayce endorsed castor oil packs as a home remedy for all kinds of problems involving lymph flow; inflammation; congestion; adhesions; constipation; gallbladder, liver, kidney and pelvic disorders; muscle spasms; chronic muscle contractions and back pain.

Caster Oil Packs

To make a pack, measure a piece of wool flannel or cotton flannel in two to three thicknesses so that it will fit over the area desired. Soak with prewarmed castor oil and apply to the body. Enclose a heating pad in plastic (or put plastic over the castor oil pack) to protect it and place over the castor oil pack where it should remain for one to one-and-a-half hours.

An abdominal pack is applied cyclically: on three days and off four days. In the following reading, Cayce advocates using the pack two or three days apart.

First, then, begin in this manner:

Every two or three days, for an hour to two hours, we would have the Castor Oil Packs over the lower portion of the liver, the gall duct, the lacteal duct, and extending to the caecum area; that is, those portions where there have been the disturbances as indicated through an engorgement of the colon itself. In these Castor Oil Packs we would use three to four thicknesses of flannel, as hot as the body can stand. These would be taken two or three days apart, for an hour at the time.

When the massage is given with the oils, let it be especially over the diaphragm area. The effect of the Castor Oil Poultice or the Castor Oil Pack is to loosen the adhesion, see? but the rubs over the area should not be too severe. All of these may be done at home. (E.C., 1055-1)

If it is used for muscle spasms, it can be applied twice a day for one and a half hours.

CAYCE MASSAGE FORMULAS

Several massage formulas are given in the Edgar Cayce readings. The following formulas, which are the most well-known, may be obtained from The Heritage Store (HS) and Home Health Products (HHP); see appendix for their addresses.

SOFT AND SMOOTH (HHP)

In reading 1968-7 this formula is given for general skin care, complexion of the face and massage to stimulate the superficial circulation and keep the body beautiful.

Peanut Oil, 6 ounces
Olive Oil, 2 ounces

Liquid Lanolin, 1 tablespoon
Rosewater, 2 ounces
This mixture absorbs easily and quickly and leaves no oily residue after a massage. As it has a short shelf life after being opened and may deteriorate after six months, it must be used up fairly quickly.

AURA GLOW (HS) & ALMOND GLOW (HHP)

A modification of the preceding formula from reading 1968-7 omits the rosewater. Vitamin E and various scents, such as lavender, almond, rose, coconut musk (HS) and jasmine, almond and coconut musk (HHP) have been added.

EGYPTIAN OIL (HS) & PENETROL (HHP)

This is recommended in reading 3363-1 as a stimulating massage for stiff muscles and joints, especially arthritis.
Add in the order named:
Usoline or Nujol (as the base), 4 ounces *(mineral oil)*
Olive Oil, 2 ounces
Peanut Oil, 2 ounces
Oil of Pine Needle, 1/2 ounce
Oil of Sassafras root, 1/2 ounce
Lanolin (liquefied), 1 ounce

GOLD RUSH (HS)

This is a very stimulating massage formula from reading 1176-1 to be used as a rubdown after the general massage is given. Cayce's directions say to pour a small quantity into an open container, dip the fingertips in and massage in just what the body will absorb.

To 2 ounces of Russian White Oil, add in the order named:
Olive Oil, 1 ounce
Cedarwood Oil, 1 ounce
Oil of Wintergreen, 1 ounce
Oil of Sassafras root, 1/3 ounce

MUSCLE TREAT (HS) & MYO RUB (HHP)

This linament formula is given in two readings, 326-5 and 243-18 (see Nujol). It will take the pain or inflammation out of the cerebrospinal system, joints, sprains, swellings or bruises, backache or injured ligaments.

To 1 ounce of Olive Oil add:
Russian White Oil, 2 ounces
Witch hazel, 1/2 ounce
Tincture of Benzoin, 1/2 ounce
Oil of Sassafras, 20 minims (drops)
Coal Oil, 6 ounces

SCARMASSAGE (HS) & SCARGO (HHP)

Daily massage once or twice a day into scars and stretch marks using this formula from reading 2015-10 stimulates circulation and brings a new skin to life. Cayce gives directions to dip the fingertips in the solution and massage it in gently so as not to produce irritation. This takes patience, persistence and perseverance and can take as long as two or two and a half years to produce the desired effects.

Mix together:
Camphorated Olive Oil, 2 ounces
Peanut Oil, 1 ounce
Lanolin (dissolved), 1/2 teaspoon
(Scargo contains beeswax as well.)

Cayce said that any scar tissue detracts from the physical health of a body because the circulation is required to continually change. However, some scars cannot be totally eradicated, such as abcesses which have been lanced.

Note: All camphor lotions should be kept out of the reach of children.

SOLE SOOTHER (HS) & SOFT STEP (HHP)

This is given in reading 555-5 for massaging tired feet, ankles and knees, and is especially good for anyone who stands on their feet a great deal.

To 4 ounces of Russian White Oil, add:
Witch hazel, 2 ounces
Rubbing alcohol, 1 ounce
Oil of Sassafras, 3-5 minims (drops)

CAMPHO-DERM (HS) & CONGESTOL (HHP)

This formula from reading 2036-6 is recommended for congestion, aches and minor pains from colds, poor circulation and kidney disorders. It is to be massaged into the chest area, lower back, lower extremities and feet. In this reading, it was also given for the congestion in the head, neck and ears.

Combine equal amounts of:

Camphor spirits

Turpentine spirits

Mutton tallow

Cayce said the mutton tallow would penetrate the skin and open the pores, thus allowing the turpentine and camphor to be absorbed.

These are only a few of the massage formulas given in the readings. Cayce's oils and formulas are an important part of the healing process as well as the hydrotherapy and massage.

_____

Endnote:

[1] In the Edgar Cayce readings, Glyco-Thymoline was a longtime recommended treatment for mucosity. Due to new FDA regulations it can only be sold today as a mouthwash and gargle. However, Cayce recommended it for many uses, such as sinus packs, a colonic solution, sunburn treatment, and many more uses too numerous to mention here. Glyco-Thymoline can be purchased in many drug stores and health food stores, and, of course, by mail-order from Home Health Products and the Heritage Store in Virginia Beach, VA. See Appendix for addresses and phone numbers.

APPENDIX

LIST OF REFERENCES

Note: The older and/or out-of-print books may be found in medical college libraries, especially chiropractic, and the National Library of Medicine.

Benjamin, Patricia J. "Is It 'Effluerage' or 'Strykning'?" *Massage Therapy Journal*. Kingsport, TN: American Massage Therapy Association, Inc., Winter, 1987.

Bohm, Max, M.D. *Massage: Its Principles and Technic*. Philadelphia & London: W.B. Saunders & Co., 1913.

Campbell, Joseph *Myths to Live By*. New York: Bantam, 1973.

Cayce, J. Gail, *Osteopathy: Comparative Concepts – A.T. Still and Edgar Cayce*. Virginia Beach, VA: Edgar Cayce Foundation, 1973.

Dychtwald, Ken, Ph.D. *Bodymind*. Los Angeles: Jeremy P Tarcher, Inc. 1950.

Greene, Elmer & Alyce, "Biofeedback & Transformation", *The American Theosophist* (May 1985) Vol. 72 No. 5.

Holmes, Thomas H., M.D. and Harold G. Wolff, M.D. "Life Situations, Emotions, and Backache," *Psychosomatic Medicine*. Vol. 14, Jan-Feb No. 1, 1952.

Kellogg, John H. *The Art of Massage*. Battle Creek, MI: Modern Medicine Publishing, Co. 1895.

King, Robert K. "From the National Director of Education," *The Massage Journal*. Kingsport, TN: American Massage Therapy Association, Inc., Summer, 1986. [Editor's note: The title of this journal changed in 1986. It is now called, *The Massage Therapy Journal*.]

Korr, Irvin, D.O. *The Collected Papers of Irvin M. Korr.* ed. Barbara Peterson. Colorado Springs, CO: American Academy of Osteopathy, 1979.

Krauss, Rosalind E. *Passages in Modern Sculpture.* Cambridge, MA: MIT Press, 1981.

Lake, Thomas T., N.D., D.C. *Treatment by Neuropathy & The Encyclopedia of Physical and Manipulative Therapeutic.* (Publisher unknown and not on title page or copyright page) 1946. [Editor's note: This is one of those obscure, out-of-print, treasures that Joseph Duggan loved. We found a copy in the Learning Resources Center of the National College Chiropractic Center in Lombard, IL. A copy is also in the National Library of Medicine.]

Maanum, Armand with Herb Montgomery, *The Complete Book of Swedish Massage.* Minneapolis, MN: Winston Press, 1985.

"Meditation, Part I: Healing Prayer and The Revelation," *The Library Series*, Vol. 2, Virginia Beach, VA: The Edgar Cayce Foundation, 1974.

McGarey, William A., M.D. *Edgar Cayce and the Palma Christi.* Virginia Beach, VA: The Edgar Cayce Foundation, 1970.

McGarey, William A., M.D. *Physicians Reference Notebook.* Virginia Beach, VA: A.R.E. Press, 1983.

McGarey, William A., M.D. *The Edgar Cayce Remedies.* New York: Bantam, 1983.

McMillan, Mary. *Massage & Therapeutic Exercise.* 3rd Ed. Philadelphia & London: W.B. Saunders, Co. 1932.

Nuernberger, Phil, Ph.D. *Freedom From Stress.* Honesdale, PA: Himalayan International Institute of Yoga Science and Philosophy, 1981.

Reilly, Harold J., D.Ph.T., D.S. and Ruth Hagy Brod. *The Edgar Cayce Handbook for Health Through Drugless Therapy.* Virginia Beach, VA: A.R.E. Press, 1987 (newest edition).

Sargent, Morgan. "Psychosomatic Backache," *The New England Journal of Medicine,* Vol. 234, No. 13, March 28, 1946.

Sarno, John, M.D. *Mind Over Back Pain.* New York: Berkeley Books, 1982.

Siegel, Bernie, M.D. *Love, Medicines & Miracles.* New York: Harper & Row, 1986.

Simonton, Carl & Stephanie. *Getting Well Again.* Los Angeles: J.P. Tarcher, 1978.

Southmayd, William, M.D. and Marshall Hoffman. "Hamstring Strains (Hamstring Pulls)," *Sports Health.* New York: Putnam Publishing Co., 1981.

Still, A.T., D.O. *Autobiography of A.T. Still.* Kirksville, MO: published by the author, 1897.

Stoddard, Alan, M.B., B.S., D.O., M.D. *Manual of Osteopathic Practice.* New York: Harper & Row, 1969.

LIST OF RESOURCES & ORGANIZATIONS

This section is intended to give you information for connecting with a part of the holistic health community, and some resources for further study.

A.R.E., Edgar Cayce Foundation & the Cayce-Reilly School of Massotherapy
67th St. & Atlantic Ave.
Virginia Beach, VA 23451

The A.R.E. Clinic
4018 N. 40th St.
Phoenix, AZ 85018

American Massage Therapy Association (AMTA)
The Massage Therapy Journal
P.O. Box 1270
Kingsport, TN 37662

Massage Magazine
P.O. Box 1389
Kailua-Kona, HI 96745

Inner Vision's
Holistic Health Updates
Box 1117M Seapines Station
Virginia Beach, VA 23451

Home Health Products
(Cayce products – This company is endorsed by the A.R.E.)
1160-A Miller Lane
Virginia Beach, VA 23451
(804) 491-2200
They accept phone orders and have a free catalog.

The Heritage Store
(Cayce products)
314 Laskin Rd.
Virginia Beach, VA 23451
(804) 428-0100
They accept phone orders and have a free catalog.

National Library of Medicine
8600 Rockville Pike
Bethesda, MD 20209

Learning Resources Center
National College Chiropractic Center
200 E. Roosevelt Road
Lombard, IL 60148

STAY IN TOUCH
AND UP TO DATE

Stay in touch through our Holistic Health Update. You'll receive periodic notices of new books and newsletters. Send your name and address to:

Inner Vision's
Holistic Health Update
Box 1117-M, Seapines Station
Virginia Beach, VA 23451

Name: _____

Company, College or Organization: _____

_____

Address: _____

City: _____ St: _____ Zip: _____

Country: _____

Type of Practice: _____

_____

EC MASSAGE